THE CAR INDUSTRY

THE CAR INDUSTRY

LABOUR RELATIONS AND INDUSTRIAL ADJUSTMENT

DAVID MARSDEN

TIMOTHY MORRIS

PAUL WILLMAN

STEPHEN WOOD

TAVISTOCK PUBLICATIONS . London and New York

First published in 1985 by
Tavistock Publications
11 New Fetter Lane, London EC4P 4EE

Published in the USA by
Tavistock Publications
in association with Methuen, Inc.
29 West 35th Street, New York NY 10001

Printed in Great Britain by
Richard Clay (The Chaucer Press) Ltd.
Bungay, Suffolk

British Library Cataloguing in Publication Data

The car industry: labour relations and industrial
   adjustment.—(Social science paperback; 313)
  1. Automobile industry and trade—Great Britain
  2. Industrial relations—Great Britain
  I. Marsden, David II. Series
  331'.0429222'0941   HD6976.A82G7
  ISBN 0–422–79550–X

Library of Congress Cataloging in Publication Data

The Car industry.
  Bibliography: p.
  Includes index.
  1. Industrial relations—Great Britain.
  2. Trade-unions—Automobile industry workers—
  Great Britain. 3. Automobile industry and trade—
  Great Britain—Management. I. Marsden, David.
  HD6976.A82G72 1985   331'.04292'0941   85–14742
  ISBN 0–422–79550–X

CONTENTS

FOREWORD

The project on which this book is primarily based was a part of the MIT Future of the Automobile Programme, and has benefited from the financial support of the Leverhulme Foundation and of the European Commission.

This project would have been impossible without the help of the numerous managers, trade union officials, and shop stewards whom we interviewed. The interviews were mostly unstructured, and often lasted several hours. In addition, many of these people commented on various drafts of our work. In all we spoke to 22 managers, 9 full-time officials, and 15 shop stewards or convenors. We wish to give them our very sincere thanks.

In the first part of the project we benefited from the collaboration of Mr Tony Manwaring and Dr Barbara Townley, both of whom contributed invaluably to the research.

In addition, we draw on data from a SERC/ERSC funded project based at Imperial College: the assistance of Mr Graham Winch is gratefully acknowledged.

This book is very much a joint effort, but overall responsibility for the main chapters was divided as follows: Chapter 1, David Marsden and Stephen Wood; Chapters 2 and 4, David Marsden; Chapter 3, Timothy Morris and Paul Willman; Chapter 5, Stephen Wood and Paul Willman; Chapter 6, Paul Willman; Chapter 7, Timothy Morris; Chapter 8, Paul Willman.

We should like to thank Dan Jones of the Science Policy

Research Unit for his encouragement throughout the project. We should also like to thank a number of people who commented on earlier material, especially David Buckle, Dave Elliott, and Mike Terry, the members of the Industrial Relations Group within the MIT project, and especially Wolfgang Streeck. Of course, the usual disclaimers apply; responsibility for any errors or inaccuracies which remain in the text lies solely with the authors.

PUBLICATIONS ARISING FROM THE MIT PROJECT

Manwaring, T. (1982) The Motor Manufacturing Industry in Britain: Prospects for the 1980s. *Industrial Relations Journal*, 14(3): 7–23.

Manwaring, T., Marsden, D. and Wood, S. (1982) Developments in Industrial Relations in the Post-War British Motor Industry. In Streeck, W. and Hoff, A. (eds) *Industrial Relations in the World Automobile Industry*. Berlin: International Institute of Management.

Marsden, D. and Wood, S. (1983) Manpower Management in the Car Industry in Britain. In Streeck, W. and Hoff, A. (eds) *Industrial Relations in the World Automobile Industry*, International Institute of Management Berlin: and Report to the Commission of the European Communities.

Marsden, D. (1985) Arbeitgeberstrategien und die Bedeutung interner Arbeitsmarkte in der Automobilindustrie. In Jacobi, O. and Kastendiek, H. (eds) *Staat und industrielle Bezeihungen in Grossbritanien*. Campus Verlag.

Marsden, D. and Wood. S. (1984) Material on Industrial Relations in the British Car Industry contributed to Altshuler, A., Anderson, M., Jones, D., Roos, D. and Womack, J. *The Future of the Automobile: the report of MIT's International Automobile Program*. London: George Allen and Unwin.

ONE
INTRODUCTION

In the middle 1970s, the British car industry showed many of the symptoms of the 'British disease' with poor productivity, bad industrial relations, and declining market shares. The only major remaining domestically owned producer, British Leyland (BL), had seen its market share halved, largely by imported cars. The multinationals producing in Britain had also suffered. Talbot's market share had undergone a similar contraction. As General Motors (GM) integrated its European operations, Vauxhall's poor performance meant that it became the junior partner in car production to its German sister company, Opel. Even Ford UK, the healthiest of the producers in the UK, did not escape the malaise as its performance compared unfavourably with that of Ford's other European operations. Against this background, the British car industry had to face several new challenges with the arrival of strong Japanese competition in domestic and export markets; increased integration and scale economies within Ford and GM, and some of the other European producers; and the advent of new production technologies. In this era of change, the British industry looked among those least able to survive.

By the middle 1980s, however, all the car producers in Britain could point to major areas in car production in which they had either eliminated or greatly reduced the gap between their own and continental European efficiency levels. At the end of 1984, BL was able to claim that its Longbridge plant, which produced the Metro, was the most efficient in Europe. How did this come about, and what were the roles of the labour force and of industrial relations?

In the late 1970s, the firms introduced a number of important changes, including new product ranges, new technologies, major reductions in employment, and continuing reform of industrial relations and working practices. In this study, we have attempted to find out how the changes in labour force organization and in industrial relations fitted into the overall problems facing the industry, and how the companies sought to tackle these. We have also sought to follow the unions' responses to these challenges, and to examine some of the implications for their future strategies.

DEVELOPMENTS IN THE MOTOR INDUSTRY

Throughout the 1970s, BL and Vauxhall and Chrysler-Talbot faced severe problems of profitability. The oil crisis in particular exposed certain weaknesses in the British car industry which went far beyond industrial relations. BL had failed to invest enough of its profits in the 1960s to develop a viable product range, rationalize its management structure following its formation, modernize its plants and machinery, or improve on the quality standards and delivery of its component suppliers.

When the world crisis of over-capacity in the motor industry intensified in the late 1970s, the various manufacturers in Britain were in very different positions, reflecting their histories and corporate identities. It is hard to generalize about the experience of the UK car industry, but all producers were by this stage already advancing on programmes to improve their position. BL underwent major internal changes, completing earlier mergers, centralizing its pay negotiations, and abandoning the old payment-by-results system for production workers. It also began collaboration with Honda. Above all else, it was seeking to develop a new and viable product range. Meanwhile, GM had increasingly integrated its British base, Vauxhall, into its world operations and had developed a strategy which would make its British plants concerned with assembly. Ford's product base was already integrated into its world car concept, and was highly profitable in Britain, profits reaching £386 million in 19 rs and was oper late 1970s all n bled from part company, Peug

Al problem, high Japan and West uality standard roductivity relat nt union— man 78 warned that y and by a large and other foreign manufacturers will continue to deteriorate'.

The acknowledged reasons for the productivity difference *vis-à-vis* most European plants included industrial relations problems in the narrow sense of the term, notably the high strike record of the industry and the way in which strikes delayed new model introduction dates. Industrial relations in a broader sense of the term was also partly responsible for other factors contributing to the low productivity, among which were relative overmanning, flexibility problems, tolerance of a high amount of lateness (and to some extent absenteeism), and 'over-generous' work standards. However, management was also at fault and was ultimately responsible for many other factors which were contributing to the low productivity. In the British-owned company, BL, the problem went right back to inadequate products, design and planning, as well as inadequate control of parts supply and working methods.

Each of the companies appears to have different priorities in seeking to adjust to the change in the automobile market despite common recognition of the problems of productivity and quality, and managers have tended to choose their angle of attack in the light of their company's external constraints, and similarly with their labour force problems. Without internally generated profits, or the backing of its parent company, or the government, Vauxhall, until the mid-1980s, had limited funds for investment in new technology and the main emphasis within its strategy has been to increase productivity and quality by improvements in management and in work organization. In contrast, BL has been able, with government support, to invest heavily in robotics on the Metro and the Maestro lines and has sought to improve its management and work practices around these new lines. Such differences, nevertheless, are essentially differences of emphasis or priority, and one should not overlook the extent to which all companies have sought greater efficiency in manning and in the organization of production.

Innovations to combat the underlying problems have included improving the design of cars so that they can be more easily produced to standard; trying to learn from other car firms, including the Japanese; improving work flow and production methods; introducing new technology; increasing the flexibility of labour within the plant; and getting and working to more realistic standards and manning levels. Whilst this book is orientated towards labour relations, all these changes will be considered, for industrial relations clearly has to be placed in the context of other changes, and the overall economic and technical context.

Of particular importance is the increasing internationalization of the industry. This process is more than simply the growth of international trade, foreign investment, and multinationals. It also involves the standardization of products and techniques on a world scale as distinctive characteristics of national markets and production techniques tend to be eliminated. It is the replacement of national norms in consumption and production, a process which is reinforced by the development of world-wide organizational structures in the multinationals and the conception of the world car. It is thus possible to speak of the creation of a world industry involving competition between firms on a world scale and the incorporation of new areas of production in the international division of labour. This process, accelerating in the 1950s with the creation of a European motor industry, had two dimensions: first, the increasing foreign penetration in the domestic markets of European producers; and second, the increased investment in European industry by US capital. Gaining momentum, this process has, since the 1970s, involved increasing investment in the semi-industrialized countries and the involvement of the Japanese manufacturers in the world markets. A further recent development of this has been capital investment by Japanese firms in the USA, and collaborative arrangements by the US manufacturers with Japanese firms.

Within this context, it is possible to locate three phases in the development of the British industry (Jones *et al.* 1983). In the first phase, which lasted until 1972/73, imports were of little importance. In the second phase (1972/73 to 1978/79) and the third phase (1979–82), they became increasingly important. The first phase was characterized by the addition of considerable production capacity, and by the mergers of almost all the UK-owned automobile producers into BLMC by 1968. The second phase began with the oil crisis, at which point demand fell, but by 1979, the end of the phase, demand had recovered to the previous 1972/73 peak. Despite this recovery UK production fell, and imports from Japan and continental Europe increased in both absolute and relative terms. During this phase, production capacity remained relatively constant and employment only declined by a relatively small amount. By contrast, in the third phase, UK production capacity was brought more in line with demand and there was an even greater reduction in the employment levels. Major plants were closed by both BL and Talbot and the increasing penetration of foreign imports continued, while BL's share of the market declined to below 20 per cent. During this period the concept of the world car became a reality, but the claimed advantages did not materialize quite as imagined. The securer foundations of BL established under Sir Michael Edwardes made the company a strong national producer able to withstand foreign competition in the long run, especially if joint ventures with foreign producers continued.

After 1982, the recovery of Vauxhall's market share, based on the J-car (Cavalier), the continued development of Ford in Europe, the success of the VW Golf, and the world-wide success of Japanese manufacturers implied that the advantages of the world car concept might again materialize. Concern for the future financing of BL at the end of 1984 implied that the small producer would always be bedevilled by the problem of financing future product development. The advantage of the world car is that this investment is spread over a far greater volume of sales.

The world car concept implies that the parts for assembly can theoretically be sourced from any part of the world. The sourcing for the Astra, one of the most recent GM models to be assembled in Britain, illustrates this well: five types of engines are used in the various versions of the car, four from Europe (West Germany or Austria) and one from Australia; glass, upholstery, front wings and steering, front doors, seat belts, and front doors from the UK; radiator and automatic transmission systems from France; and the manual gearbox from Japan or Austria.

THE ROLE OF INDUSTRIAL RELATIONS

Such developments in the industry imply that industrial relations cannot be given primacy in explaining company or national performance, although Britain's labour problems have long been associated with the overall problem of the economy in the minds of businessmen, politicians, and the media. The motor industry, and particularly British Leyland, became the prime example of this British disease. With the collapse of BLMC in the early 1970s and the continual public concern about the industry, three major inquiries were conducted in the mid-1970s into the industry: the Ryder Report, being specifically on BL, the House of Commons Expenditure Committee (1975), and the Central Policy Review Staff (1975) covering the whole industry. All three put weight on the bad working practices which obstructed efficient capital utilization, although they, and particularly the Ryder Report, also emphasized the age and inferiority of the capital stock, inadequate product development, and poor and badly integrated management at BL. Despite this and other acknowledgements that the industry's problems were not simply labour problems, the restrictive practices and particularly excessive strikes continued to preoccupy public discussion of the industry and prompted companies to continue their quest to reduce manning levels or close plants. In the mid-1980s, despite high levels of unemployment, companies remain aware of their work-forces' power and of the consequent need for their co-operation, so that industrial relations remains central to each firm's competitive position.

Nevertheless, given the importance of other factors in the motor industry in the 1970s, some writers such as Williams *et al.* (1983) have concluded that the emphasis on industrial relations is misplaced. According to them the problems of the British motor industry relate, especially in BL and Talbot, to past failings in management, product development, and capital utilization, whereas all other problems – strikes, working practices, and manning levels – are secondary. But it is one thing to argue that industrial relations is just one factor contributing to company performance, it is another to argue that it plays no role. The problems of industrial relations must be set in the context of the other factors, which is precisely what managements have done. A weakness of the Williams *et al.* argument is that it neglects the very real sense in which labour relations has been a core element of the firms' strategies, as we shall see in the next chapter. Managers do not simply associate labour relations problems with worker performance, as if workers alone are to blame or are insensitive to the requirements of changing competitive conditions. Many of the reports within the industry on the productivity gap between British plants and their foreign rivals identify managerial responsibilities. An important part, for example, of Ford's overall corporate philosophy has always been a stress on managerial prerogatives and the need for managers to manage, with the implication that bad labour relations ultimately reflect bad management. In the motor industry managers operate with a number of key assumptions, an important one of which is that having cars in the showroom and fulfilling delivery dates is vital to the achievement of sales, for customers in the mass markets shop around and make their decisions largely on the basis of what is available at the time. In the more specialist markets again delivery is vital, especially where, as in the case of Land Rover, customers buy in bulk for specific purposes, fulfilment of which cannot be postponed. Management also operates with the view that purchasing decisions and particularly the maintenance of customer loyalty and repeat orders is affected by the company's image and, particularly in the case of British manufacturing in the 1970s, by poor industrial relations. The collapse of the British market in Scandinavia is often used to support this argument. Management are particularly sensitive to the potential problem of protracted negotiations when new products are introduced which affect their rates of output 'climb' and profitability during their first year of production. Another very important cause for concern is the potential effect of poor labour discipline and motivation on quality.

Managers break the industrial relations problem down into a number of elements, as we shall see to some extent in Chapters 2 and 5. An important element of all the companies' approach to Japanese competition has been their belief that, in terms of industrial engineering and technology, they are not behind their West European and Japanese competitors. Ford managers claim that there has never been much difference in the actual line speeds or standards between the various European plants. A good deal of the productivity gap arises from interruptions to the line. The changes in industrial relations which managements have sought to effect have thus been targeted at specific problems and consequently have involved more than procedural changes or a simple 'roll back' of shop steward power. The crude association of the managements' industrial relations strategy with a stereotyped conception of 'macho management' is far too simplistic, as we shall see.

THE STRUCTURE OF THE BOOK

The main body of the book begins with a chapter outlining the economic changes in the industry, the managerial strategies adopted by the companies in the light of these, and their implications for their industrial relations strategies. In Chapter 3 the role of technical change in the firms' strategies will be considered and the implications of these developments assessed. In Chapter 4 the changes in the quantity and type of employment in the industry are discussed and the question of whether a new type of work-force, one more dependent on their current employer, is being formed will be examined. The nature of the changing working practices and the strategies adopted by management to foster them will be the subject of Chapter 5. In Chapter 6, an attempt to assess the overall thrust of the changes discussed in the previous chapters will be made, and particular attention will be paid to their impact on the industry's strike record. In Chapter 7, the trade union strategies towards the changes discussed thus far will be outlined and here the implications of the internationalization of the industry for trade unionism will be of particular concern, especially given the decentralized nature of the British trade union movement. The book concludes with an overview of the developments in the industry and makes some tentative assessments of the likely developments in labour relations.

The focus of the main chapters will be on issues related specifically to the motor industry. More general issues to which these are related will be reserved for the final chapter. It may, though, be useful to refer to some of these at this stage. First, there is the question of the role of industrial relations in Britain's economic performance. According to some recent critics industrial relations is of negligible importance alongside other factors, such as the level of investment and managerial competence. The excessive preoccupation in the media with industrial relations should be put in perspective, yet, as we have already said, the importance of industrial relations should not be denied. The successful pursuit by management of productivity gains in the early 1980s provides us with a situation for testing the role of industrial relations; for if industrial relations is of little or no importance these productivity changes will not reflect any industrial relations changes, and by implication could have been achieved in their absence. According to alternative perspectives, any fundamental break with the relatively low productivity levels of the past must involve a radical change in strategy away from the past emphasis on hierarchical control. So the second general question concerns the nature of the new managerial initiative: is it an attempt to increase employee involvement and devolve power or a toughening up by management, the kind of 'macho management' associated with Sir Michael Edwardes at BL from 1977–81.

This raises the thi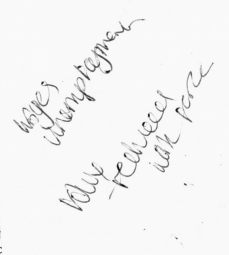
of collective bargaini
introduction of chan
working practices hav
car industry in a clii
the increasingly high
government's attitude
example, the facilitie
involvement in many
But many of the char
negotiation with worl
union officials. At For
changes did not require
only a firmer implemen
fundamental changes, a
framework of manager
Improved working prac
and associated with the .... and products, as for example with the Metro line at Long-bridge.

The fourth question is indeed the relationship between technology and work organization, that is the extent to which the former is the main determinant of the latter, or whether management have a considerable scope for their choice of work organization under any given technology. The fifth question concerns the reductions of employment and union responses. Manpower reductions have occurred in all firms. Both BL and Vauxhall reduced their work-force by about one-third between 1979 and 1983. Whilst BL has made closures and company reorganizations which have demanded redundancies, many of their separations, like all those at Ford, Vauxhall, and Talbot, have been on a voluntary basis. Although there has been little or no overt struggle against the plant closures, the main expression of union concern has continued to be the loss of jobs, and especially in BL, with what they perceive to be a loss of their power, an autocratic management style, and increasing effort levels. The recent S-car dispute with Vauxhall is an expression of the former where the trade unions were negotiating not so much to stop the S-car from being produced in Spain, but to limit the number of other cars entering the country from other parts of Europe, a demand which to some extent they successfully achieved. The early finishing dispute in March 1983 at Cowley is an example of the second kind of discontent, where the workers and their representatives were basically complaining about the way management was treating them.

The changes within the motor industry have brought about considerable improvements in productivity and quality. They have been introduced in a climate of crisis, often with an implication that without acceptance of them all jobs within the industry will go, and perhaps even that success could be greeted with a feeling of improved job security.

So the sixth question raised is the extent to which the increasing concern with Japanese methods involves a move towards a commitment to some kind of lifetime employment or job security. Several factors might cause a move in this direction. Technical change has led to alterations in traditional job boundaries creating bundles of skills which are less easily transferred to other employers, and the increased emphasis on flexibility of deployment within the firm may require some commitment from the companies to offer more stable employment in return. However, there has been no equivalent in Britain to the agreements at Ford and GM in the USA on employment security. Nevertheless, the industry is of interest to those concerned with the world-wide vogue for Japanese management, as all four companies have attempted to adapt features of this as they have reacted to challenge from Japanese competition.

A last and related point is indeed the increasing internationalization of the industry and its implications for employment levels and industrial relations, including the very concept of national systems. Throughout this book we have been acutely conscious of the problems of focusing on a nation, that is on the British car industry when it is so clearly also part of the American and French industries, and will become part of the

Japanese industry in 1986. It is this dimension of the development of the car industry with which any consideration of managerial strategy and industrial relations must begin, and hence where our next chapter starts.

TWO
MANAGEMENT
STRATEGY

THE PROBLEMS FACING THE COMPANIES IN BRITAIN

A gradual rise in oil prices from the 1980s, owing to depletion of cheaper oil sources, could have been foreseen by the car producers, but as it had none of the drama of the oil price hikes of 1973 and 1979, and did not call for such a rapid readjustment of the types of cars produced, they were not prepared. The sharpness of the oil price rises also caused rapid readjustment of industrial economies, and had a sharp deflationary effect which was exacerbated in a number of countries by government economic policies designed to restrain the inflation set in motion by the oil price rises. This also affected the demand for cars. Thus car producers in the 1970s were caught between the need to adapt their models to new customer demands and the sharp deflationary effects of the oil price rises.

The change of economic conditions did not hit all car producing countries equally, and within countries some firms were better placed than others. During the 1970s, Britain was one of the countries to suffer most from increased competition from imports: the share of imports rose from 10 per cent of the new car market in 1969 to 35 per cent by 1977, after which

Table 1 *Shares of the British car market of the main producers 1970–84*

year	BL	Ford	Vauxhall	Chrysler/ Talbot	Datsun/ Nissan/ Honda/ Toyota	others (mostly imported)	UK new car registra- tion (000)[a]
1970	38.1	26.5[b]	10.0	11.2[b]	0.4	13.8	91.4
1971	40.2	18.7	10.8	12.4	1.0	16.9	108.5
1972	33.1	24.5	9.0	11.4	2.9	19.1	138.6
1973	31.9	22.6	8.0	11.5	5.1	20.9	137.1
1974	32.7	22.7	7.3	10.8	6.1	20.4	102.8
1975	30.9	21.7	7.4	8.0	7.9	24.1	98.5
1976	27.4	25.3	8.9	6.4	8.1	23.9	106.5
1977	24.3	25.7	9.1	6.0	9.1	25.8	109.4
1978	23.5	24.7	8.2	7.1	9.4	27.5	131.6
1979	19.6	28.3	8.2	7.0	8.9	28.0	142.0
1980	18.2	30.7	8.8	6.0	9.8	26.5	126.6
1981	19.2	30.9	8.6	4.6	8.6	28.1	124.5
1982	17.8	30.5	11.7	3.6	8.8	27.6	132.0
1983	18.2	28.9	14.6	4.4	8.7	25.2	148.9
1984	18.3[c]	27.8	16.2	4.0	9.0	24.7	147.4

Sources: SMMT, and Economic Trends.
Notes: a. monthly averages; b. Ford Europe only 1970–72, and Chrysler France and Chrysler UK only 1970–72; c. including Jaguar.

its growth slowed markedly (*Table 1*). The most dramatic component was the increase in the share of the Japanese producers – Datsun, Honda, and Toyota – from almost nothing in 1970 to nearly 10 per cent of the market by 1980. The greater part of this increased share of imports was at the expense of BL, whose market share dropped from 40 per cent in 1969 to under 20 per cent by 1979, and of Chrysler/Talbot, whose share fell from 11 per cent in 1970 to under 5 per cent by 1981. Ford took over as market leader from BL in 1977, but it only filled part of the gap left by BL and Chrysler/Talbot, having itself lost market share between 1972 and 1975. In addition, British car production for export fell from over 60,000 vehicles in 1970 to about 40,000 in 1978, and under 20,000 by 1982.

At first sight it would seem that the crisis of the British car industry was first and foremost a crisis of its only major domestically owned producer, BL, but this would be to neglect the important changes in the composition of output at the three multinationals, especially Vauxhall and Talbot. In addition to changes in UK market share, the foreign content in the cars produced by these two firms in Britain was greatly increased. Thus by the 1980s, both Vauxhall and Talbot were mostly assembling cars in the UK whose parts had been manufactured elsewhere. This was partly because of increased Europe-wide integration of operations by the multinationals, but there was also a deeper problem of efficiency in the industry in Britain which meant that international integration worked on the whole against Britain. That Ford UK did not wholly escape this crisis is clear from its inability to take full advantage of the contraction of BL's market share in the mid-1970s.

The other major threat which compounded this crisis was the arrival of Japanese competition, which built up from the early 1970s and affected European and North American car markets. Its impact was most visible in markets in the smaller European countries with no native car producers to press for restrictions on Japanese imports. This was most strongly felt in the late 1970s as Ford and GM found themselves under severe pressure from the Japanese in these unprotected markets despite the cost of shipping Japanese cars halfway round the world. Altshuler *et al.* (1984: Fig. 7.1) show that between 1975 and 1980 the Japanese producers had made enormous gains in efficiency. Adjusting for the typical car being produced, and including hours of management, clerical labour, and suppliers, they showed that in 1975 it took the Japanese about 200 hours to build a vehicle, but by 1980 this had fallen to about 140 hours. In contrast, West German producers remained at their 1976 level, taking between 190 and 210 hours, while the Americans went from about 190 hours in 1975 to about 205 hours in 1980. According to the authors, these figures overstate the number of hours used in Japan, and understate those for the USA and West Germany. Even allowing for the increased complexity of the West German and American cars, the contrast between the trends for Japan and the other two countries is considerable.

In the late 1970s it seemed that the industry would be dominated by the 'world car' concept, namely that there were major economies of scale in production and development work which could only be achieved by reaching a significant market share in several countries using variants of the same basic model. At the same time, the car producers could draw on different countries' strength and cost advantages in certain areas of car production. This was the philosophy behind Ford's new Escort, and GM's 'J-car', the Cavalier, introduced in 1980 and 1981 respectively. Against this background it was hard to see how smaller volume producers, heavily reliant upon their own national markets, could survive.

In the event, smaller producers have been able to survive by taking advantage of economies of scale in certain areas, for example buying in key components from larger producers. BL now uses VW and Honda gearboxes in the Maestro and the Montego, and has been involved in a number of joint ventures with Honda, especially with the new executive car. The two firms have been deeply involved together in its concept, design, and style, and have combined to engineer, manufacture, and sell the car world-wide.

In addition, technical change, although requiring immense economies of scale for the development of new production technology, may be reducing the minimum efficient scale in certain areas of manufacture. Whereas the technology of even the middle 1970s required great amounts of dedicated capital equipment, the introduction of reprogrammable robots, given sufficient flexibility in the organization of production, could enable smaller companies to produce a range of variations on a standard model, thus enabling them to reach more levels of the market with the same basic model, as Malsch, Dohse, and Jurgens (1984) have argued in connection with BMW.

The rise of the Japanese producers has displaced the British producers from former export markets. In the UK, its main impact on the market was in the light to medium range of cars, for example with the Datsun Sunny and Cherry. Their impact on the UK market has been attenuated by voluntary import quotas which were fairly rapidly negotiated, limiting Japanese sales in Britain to under 11 per cent of the market. In addition, they had no incentive to reduce price in order to extend their market share, so that they could enjoy most of their efficiency advantage in the form of higher profit margins.

The system of voluntary quotas has left the European and American producers a chance to restructure, to improve their efficiency, and to develop new models, but it has also given rise to a number of moves by Japanese companies to gain greater access by other means, such as the joint ventures already mentioned, and the establishment of production facilities in Britain and the USA, such as the Nissan factory in north-east England.

For the future of employment in the industry in Britain there was the additional problem that both Ford and GM could claim that they could produce cars more cheaply in other European countries, notably West Germany, whose higher efficiency levels more than compensated for the labour cost differential, and Spain and Portugal. The unit labour cost differential within the multinationals became an increasingly important problem for Britain as they integrated their European operations from the mid-1970s.

THE ADJUSTMENT PROBLEM FACING THE CAR FIRMS

By the late 1970s Ford had already integrated its European operations with the establishment of Ford Europe in 1967, which was followed by the production of common models in Britain and West Germany, starting with the Capri in 1969 and the Cortina in 1970. These were designed jointly and assembled in both Britain and West Germany. In 1978, the Fiesta was produced in Dagenham, Saarlouis, and Valencia; the Cortina in Dagenham and Genk; and the Escort in Halewood and Saarlouis. Although GM had plants in Britain (Luton and Ellesmere Port), West Germany (Bochum and Russelsheim), and Belgium (Antwerp), in the late 1970s only the West German and Belgian plants were fully integrated. Vauxhall was a more or less independent entity. Bhaskar (1979) has argued that one reason for the later integration of its European operations was that GM believed that the differences between individual European markets were such that nationally based plants had adequate economies of scale. However, Ford's successful development of Europe-wide models had given the lie to this by the early 1980s. With the experience of lower productivity than the German plants, and of losses throughout the 1970s, the Vauxhall end of GM's European car operation was bound to become the junior partner when they were integrated.

In the late 1970s, BL's position was more precarious. The company had been the fruit of moves to rationalize the British-owned car industry in the 1960s and 1970s. For a considerable time, manufacturing capacity was not rationalized, and the company entered the 1970s with a number of competing model ranges, and rivalry between the management teams of the old companies. In contrast with Ford and Vauxhall, the British-owned company had to forge its own corporate identity and integrated management structure. This problem of identity also lay at the heart of some of BL's labour problems as it owned a number of plants with different traditions of management and labour relations, and different methods of payment and work organization. One of its biggest problems in the 1970s was to develop greater central control over wage bargaining in order to reduce the dangers of 'leap-frogging' between plants and consequent strikes.

Again in contrast with Ford and GM, BL's attempts to develop as a multinational, with plants in Belgium, Italy, and Spain, foundered in the crisis the company encountered in 1973–74 with the sale of Innocenti to the Italian state agency GEPI, and of the Spanish Authi plant to Seat. Apart from the Mini, it also had a model range in the early 1970s which was not appropriate for European markets, and in this period it lost many of its dealer networks on the continent. Moreover, it could not call upon its operations in Germany or elsewhere to fill the model gap in the way Vauxhall could with the Cavalier, whose development work was done outside the UK. On the other hand, once taken into public ownership in 1975, it could call upon government funds through the National Enterprise Board (NEB) to assist with development work.

The problems at Chrysler/Talbot were exacerbated by the economic difficulties of the parent company in the USA in the mid-1970s, which led Chrysler's American management to present the British government with an ultimatum in 1976 – to take over its British operations, or it would close them within three months. In 1978, Chrysler UK was taken over by the

French group Peugeot-Citroen, which revived the Talbot name for the former Chrysler operations in Britain and France. Although Talbot's UK plants were fairly new, productivity levels compared unfavourably with Peugeot-Citroen's other plants with productivity levels between two-thirds and three-quarters of Citroen world-wide (Bhaskar 1979).

Table 2 *Pre-tax profit/loss of the companies in the UK 1975–82* (*£ millions*)

year	BL	Ford	Vauxhall	Chrysler/Talbot
1970–74 (an. ave)	24.3	23.0	(38.9)	(4.5)
1975	(76.1)	14.0	(12.8)	(35.5)
1976	70.5	122.0	(1.7)	(42.6)
1977	3.1	246.0	(2.0)	(21.5)
1978	1.7	242.0	2.0	(20.2)
1979	(112.2)	386.0	(31.7)	(41.1)
1980	(387.5)	226.0	(83.3)	(75.1)
1981	(332.9)	220.0	(57.4)	(91.0)
1982	(222.7)	194.0	(37.9)	(54.9)
1983	(67.1)	178.0	(1.0)	3.1
1984				

Source: Company reports, five- and ten-year summary statistics sections, and Fourteenth Report of the Expenditure Committee (Session 1974–75).

Notes: Vauxhall 1983 excludes commercial vehicles division sold to GM Overseas on 31 December, 1982.

Of the three companies, only Ford made a consistent profit on its operations in Britain over the period, Vauxhall and Chrysler/Talbot making a loss throughout almost all the decade (*Table 2*). BL's profit position was fair by comparison until 1978, but from 1979 its position deteriorated very rapidly.

Thus each of the companies went into the crisis of the late 1970s and early 1980s from very different commercial positions. They nevertheless faced a number of common problems arising from conditions in Britain, and the inability of either multinational to run its operations as efficiently and with the same quality of output as in their continental European plants. For example, according to Ford, in 1977 owner-reported problems per 100 cars for their models produced in Britain were roughly twice those for their German-produced models. For the Fiesta the figures were 242 compared with 142; for the Escort, 256 compared with 125 (Bhaskar 1979: 144).

To summarize, the problem facing the British car industry in the late 1970s was a mixture of the depth of the recession in all the major economies, compounded by the large efficiency advantage that the Japanese producers had developed by the 1970s in relation to their European and North American competitors. Britain faced the additional problem of poor productivity and quality as compared with other European producers. This affected all the major companies producing in Britain, and was compounded by the crisis of BL, the former market leader, and Chrysler/Talbot, whose losses of market share were largely made up by imports from the continent and especially from Japan. In addition, there was a decline in the UK domestic content of Ford and especially Vauxhall cars.

THE PROBLEM OF COMMERCIAL AND COST STRATEGY

The problem of cost and of commercial strategy was most acute with BL by the mid-1970s. The Mini was in need of updating, and BL was losing market share badly on its other models. It had little alternative to developing a new and more competitive model range, and to pitch this at competitive prices. Sir Michael Edwardes sought to achieve this by cutting a good deal of its existing plants and capacity. BL had also to update and retool its remaining plants, and to increase efficiency of organization and of manning. But unless its new models were right for the market, these other changes would not have halted the company's decline. As Jones (1985) stressed, the development of the new models was the longest range part of BL's strategy for survival. The new Mini, the Austin Metro, was the first of the new models. Work began on it in earnest in 1976, and it was launched in 1980, followed by the Maestro in 1983, the Montego in 1984, the new Honda-designed Rover in 1984, and the executive car in 1985. As a stop-gap, the Acclaim was introduced from Honda, enabling BL to maintain a presence in the medium car segment of the market in the early 1980s.

Decisions on the new model range influenced a number of the subsequent decisions, such as the concentration of production facilities on two main plants at Longbridge, the old Austin plant, and at Cowley, the old Morris plant. These then were the plants that were progressively to be retooled, the most dramatic and widely publicized step being the setting up of the robot welders on the new Metro line at Longbridge in 1979. BL's future survival in many respects depended upon success on each of these points: without better models they could not hope to regain market share, and without the modernization of facilities, improvements in quality, and the changes in organization and working practices they could not get the selling price competitive.

Whereas BL's strategy was based mainly on survival in the British market, for Ford and GM, Britain provided a large market, in which they owned substantial facilities, but their position in Britain was only part of a wider strategy. Unlike BL, if their plans went wrong in Britain, they still had very important markets on the continent and in the USA, although to some extent in the late 1970s and early 1980s Ford needed profits from its British operations to support its recovery in the USA. Japanese import penetration was considerably higher there than in Europe. Nevertheless, the scale of investment of new models, such as GM's J-car, or Ford's Escort or Sierra, was rather greater than BL could afford, and the stakes were correspondingly higher. Moreover, if their reorganization plans for their facilities in the UK failed, they could always increase the extent to which they supplied the British market from their continental plants, although there are wider political limits on the extent to which this can be done.

Although Ford, and to a much lesser extent GM, have maintained their British facilities, since 1975 the local content of the cars they sell on the British market has declined. Jones (1985) estimated that the local content of both Ford and Vauxhall car sales in the UK declined on a value basis between 1975 and 1979; whereas BL had a 93 per cent local content in 1983, the corresponding figures for Ford and Vauxhall were 47 per cent and 26 per cent respectively. In terms of units sold, domestic contents were 100 per cent for BL, and 54 per cent and 47 per cent respectively for Ford and Vauxhall. GM exports few cars from Britain, so that the decline in domestic content reveals its reduced reliance upon its UK production facilities. Nevertheless, GM's recent investment in modernizing the Vauxhall plants at Ellesmere Port and Luton, and its readiness to maintain UK production facilities despite recurrent losses might be taken as evidence of continued commitment to production in the UK. Ford continues to use its UK facilities as part of its integrated European production, and continues to export from the UK albeit as a smaller net exporter than in earlier years.

Neither Ford nor Vauxhall have anything like the same dependence upon success in production in the UK and in the UK car market as BL. Nevertheless, as they maintain production facilities in the UK, simply as the price to be paid for access to one of the largest European car markets, these two companies have had to press for greater efficiency in their UK facilities. Particularly for Ford, the British plants are part of an integrated European production system on whose overall cost efficiency Ford depends in order to compete successfully in European markets, notably with GM and the Japanese. Inefficiency in its British plants would drag down the overall performance of its European operations.

In addition, the introduction of new models by all the major producers has created opportunities for an extra dimension of competition by taking advantage of the fall in price of micro-electronically controlled equipment. The advantage of this new technology in terms of improved quality control and of possible labour saving is such that the firms have had little alternative but to introduce it on new models; but to be used to maximum effect, as argued in Chapter 3, it requires a fairly radical reorganization of production.

LABOUR MANAGEMENT IN RELATION TO COMMERCIAL AND COST STRATEGY

One of the major innovations underlying the Japanese surge of efficiency during the 1970s had been the perfection of the 'just in time' system production co-ordination. This means that component suppliers should deliver the goods only hours before they were due to be assembled, and that buffer stocks should be reduced to a bare minimum. But reducing buffer stocks requires a high degree of predictability in production flow and a special relationship with suppliers. One of the chief reasons for high levels of buffer stocks in British car plants during the 1970s had been to create the slack necessary to enable line managers to keep production flowing despite a large number of interruptions at different points in the production process. These interruptions could arise for many reasons, including bad planning and poor organization, local bottlenecks and industrial disputes at component suppliers, and at various points on the line. The price of these additional stocks was poor utilization of factory space and the capital tied up in spares. In addition, planning for bottlenecks exacerbated an already poor system of labour utilization as people were needed to move the stocks around, and on stand-by. To reduce buffer stocks clearly required a major change in the pattern of work-force organization, and in labour relations.

A second major problem facing the producers was the gap in quality of output between Britain and Japan, but also between Britain and the rest of Europe. Quality is important for the reputation of the final product, and there were times in the 1970s when Ford could only sell its German and not its British-produced models in Sweden because of quality problems. But it is also an important source of additional production costs because of the man-hours lost in tracing faulty work and in subsequent rectification. Extra lines were needed for rectification in many plants.

Quality control is partly a question of equipment, but it is also a question of the attitudes of the work-force, and of the state of labour–management relations. In complex assembly work it is practically impossible for management to check every single piece of work, so for many operations the work-force has to be trusted. Poor quality can also be the result of inadequate training, particularly if new recruits learn the job from more experienced workers who may not themselves have been shown what the correctly assembled item looks like. High rates of labour turnover intensify such problems, and although turnover is influenced by labour market conditions, it is also affected by the state of work relations.

Another source of 'over-manning' can be rigid or narrow job descriptions. These can be the result of management policy, such as an over-emphasis upon specialization. For example, it had been common in the technician area to insist upon an unnecessarily high degree of specialization, and indeed the whole philosophy of work on the production line was that work tasks should be highly specialized. But they are often also the result of restrictive practices and the use of bargaining over job boundaries.

A final aspect of inefficient utilization of labour, as of other resources, is that efficiency is a relative and not an absolute concept. It has economic significance mostly in relation to the performance of firms competing in the same markets. Thus one company's method of labour utilization only becomes disadvantageous when a competitor finds other methods which give rise to a cost or quality advantage. It is of the nature of such changes that neither the management nor the workers are immediately aware that their own established and tested methods have become relatively less efficient. Many of them will never have been inside the innovating plant.

Thus an important part of the drive to improve efficiency has involved making both managers and workers aware of such changes. BL's special joint productivity sub-committee, set up in 1976 to study productivity in BL compared to other European plants, was one such exercise.

The productivity comparisons

A number of detailed analyses of the productivity problems of the British car industry were carried out in the mid to late 1970s, and although their primary focus was BL where the concern was greatest, they highlighted problems also existing in the other firms.

In March 1976, under the participation scheme at Leyland Cars, a joint productivity sub-committee consisting of senior shop stewards and management was set up 'to make recommendations to the Joint Management Council of Leyland Cars on the improvement of all aspects of productivity in Leyland car plants, such recommendations being designed for use by Plant Participation Committees'. Under this committee comparisons were made between BL plants and plants of Renault, VW, and Simca-Chrysler, as well as between BL's UK and Belgian plants. They dealt with five main problems: work practices; manning and motivation; management and supervision; materials (including stocks); and machines, plant, and equipment. The sub-committee broke down the poor productivity of the BL plants as follows.

Table 3 *Productivity comparison Leyland-Europe.*

	BL		European
Effective work-force availability (% of working year)	72		80
	unadjusted	adjusted	
achievement of manned capacity			
power train	83	74	98
body and assembly	72	61	98
output per operator VW as base = 100%			
power train	75	67	95
body and assembly	56	48	97
use of time at work (productive)			
power train	60	53	79
body and assembly	44	38	80

Source: Report of the Productivity Sub-committee of the Joint Management Council of Leyland Cars, 1978.
Notes: Comparisons done for a medium-sized car. Continental plants – Renault, Flins and Cleon; VW, Wolfsburg and Salzgitter; and Simca-Chrysler, Poissy. Data for mid-1970s.
Unadjusted figures: based on current time standards.
Adjusted figures: based on specially estimated standards – same for all plants.

The reasons that they identified for the shortfall in BL's plants (which are discussed more fully in Chapter 5) included a higher rate of industrial disputes, higher relaxation allowances, higher allowed non-productive time (which was often exceeded), and work standards and manning levels that were in need of revision. The unadjusted figures were based on current time standards, and the adjusted figures on time standards specially estimated by independent industrial engineers for the exercise, and when compared to the unadjusted figures shows that part of the productivity differential was due to differences in the standards in use. Although there were some marked differences between plants, none of Leyland's UK plants approached the levels of efficiency in the continental plants, nor even that of BL's Belgian plant in Seneffe.

These comparisons relate to BL only, and are not necessarily reflective of conditions in the other companies. According to the House of Commons Select Committee (1975), BL was the weakest of the producers in the UK in the mid-1970s. Taking value added per employee as a percentage of the UK average for the industry, in 1974 Ford was in the strongest position with productivity 41 per cent above the UK average, then came Chrysler UK on the average, with Vauxhall 8 per cent below average, and BL 23 per cent below. The dispersion between the producers in West Germany was smaller, with the average for the industry there 83 per cent above the UK level at current exchange rates. Renault also compared favourably with all the producers in the UK.

However, the advantageous position of Ford UK slipped, at least in its Halewood plant by comparison with its sister plant in Saarlouis. According to a Ford newsletter to its Halewood employees in 1983, labour and overhead efficiency in Halewood declined by 15 per cent between 1972 and 1978 while Saarlouis underwent continuous improvement of 41 per cent between 1972 and 1982. One of the striking features of the Saarlouis improvement was its continuous nature year on year. Indeed, in the same newsletter Ford showed how from a position in the mid-1970s in which both Halewood and Saarlouis had each supplied the Escort for export to about seven or eight national markets, by 1983 Halewood was supplying only two, Ireland and Italy, while Saarlouis was supplying thirteen.

Ford and Vauxhall have made extensive use of productivity comparisons between their British and the continental plants, the aim being not so much to alarm their British work-forces as to help their British management identify the ways in which productivity improvements might be achieved. The problem of non-productive time was also highlighted in the comparison of performance between Ford's two plants producing the Escort, Halewood and Saarlouis. Although output varies in response to expected sales, Ford management pointed out that over the seven years between 1976 and 1982 Halewood was working on average at about two-thirds capacity.

By the late 1970s, further scope for reducing unit costs by reducing relative pay in the industry was more or less exhausted. Weekly pay levels in the industry compared to the rest of British manufacturing industry fell from 18 per cent above the average for manual men in 1972 to only 6 per cent above in 1979, and 5 per cent above in 1984. Further reduction in relative pay would entail major changes in the type of labour employed in the industry. Even then the scope would be limited as one of the main causes of differences in pay between the car industry in different countries lies in average efficiency levels across the whole economy, or at least across the whole of the traded sector. Consequently, improved efficiency offers much greater scope for long-run reduction in unit costs. In any case, Britain is among the lower wage cost producers, with hourly compensation costs per employee in 1979 less than half those of the USA and West Germany, and well below those of France, Italy, and Japan (US Department of Labor, Bureau of Labor Statistics). But the differences were mostly offset by Britain's lower output per head.

Except for wholesale plant closures, demanning requires an extensive reorganization of jobs and of working practices, the negotiation of which is very complex. Looking behind the causes of non-productive time picked out by the BL Joint Management Committee is quite revealing. They pointed to greater allowed non-productive time; excess over allowed non-productive time; disputes; rest allowances; and lower work standards in that order. Work standards are calculated by the industrial engineers, the standard comprising basic minutes plus the relaxation allowance. This is then discussed with the financial analysts and production supervisors so that an allowed or budgeted off-standard time can be agreed. This makes allowances for variations in the quality of parts to be assembled requiring some rectification, damaged parts due to inadequate storage facilities; the retention of old plant and machinery; and the time required to repair breakdowns. Some of these are management organization problems, but others are industrial relations problems. For example, time spent on repair work is based on existing manning and work practices within maintenance departments, and thus on skill demarcations. The impact of some of these is hard to predict, and may be increased by, for example, extended relaxation time, agreed late starts and early finishes, materials shortages occurring more frequently than allowed for, difficulty of redeploying labour which has no work on its own, and output reduction owing to industrial action short of a strike. Better organization and tighter management discipline can reduce some of these, but such discipline is usually most effective when it is accepted as legitimate by the work-force and the unions. Similarly difficulty of redeploying labour can be an industrial relations problem, while the last one mentioned could be a problem of inadequate use of procedures for settling disputes.

The BL sub-committee thought that poor industrial relations contributed to a high level of non-productive time. Disputes clearly also fell into this category, and reduction of rest allowances would usually require negotiation in the same way as would a reduction in pay.

The only items which might appear to be independent of industrial relations were the work standards themselves. But it is clear that there is no hard and fast distinction between the job as planned and the existing set of working practices. Standard times take account of existing job demarcations, and so to some extent embody established working practices.

THE POSITION OF LABOUR MANAGEMENT IN CORPORATE PLANNING

For each of the companies, product strategy lay at the centre of their planning, but because car assembly remains a fairly labour-intensive activity, labour costs, and thus efficiency of labour utilization, are a major factor. But this does not tell us much about how manpower and industrial relations decisions fit into the commercial decisions. The three main areas in which thinking ahead about labour are critical are those of training, working practices, and industrial relations practices.

Each of the three big companies has a fairly similar process of ten-year rolling corporate plans, with more detailed five-year and shorter period rolling plans in any year. The main purpose of these is not to decide now what should be done for the next ten years, but to establish a framework within which decisions with differing time horizons can be fixed, and to analyse different options. The ten-year plans would look at such items as product development, volumes, capacity, and manpower levels, with detailed finance being worked out five years ahead. Not all long-term decisions however relate to models. A good example would be Ford's decision to standardize engine and other components across models, which is something that can only be introduced gradually. Within the framework of ten- and five-year plans, BL also uses a system of project teams, such as for a new model, or a model face-lift. In a period of expansion a more piecemeal approach to planning might be possible, but at BL, for example, concern for fuller capacity utilization has led to much more systematic thinking about the interrelations between different decisions. For example, in order to eliminate the problems created by temporary labour surpluses and to ease retraining, it is necessary to be more careful about the effect of timing of the introduction of new models upon the different plants. Consequently, training has come to play a more important part in the five-year plans because of the need to deploy training resources in good time.

Training

Planning of certain training needs is to some extent eased by the existence of a fairly large labour market in engineering skills on which the companies can draw. But the emphasis in training in recent years has broadened away from formal training of apprentices to greater use of training of semi-skilled workers in order to improve quality, and to retraining, partly because of its role in keeping down redundancies, and partly in order to increase flexibility of deployment as discussed in Chapter 4. Whereas in earlier years the companies could perhaps gear their training to contributing to a general pool of skilled labour on their local labour markets from which they and other employers could draw as they needed, subject to the perennial problem of skill shortages in a boom, training for quality and for redeployment has meant that training has come to play a more strategic role in forward planning. Thus, even though the lead times of the training may be shorter in training for quality and redeployment than for apprenticeships, the training department has sought to anticipate future needs. Consequently, it has come to play a larger role in the companies' forward thinking, although it remains a long way downstream from the strategic decisions on product development.

Working practices

The position of working practices in the companies' long-term planning has depended in part upon the extent to which these were a problem for the individual companies. BL's problems were perhaps the most serious of all the companies in the early 1970s, and were in part responsible for its low productivity position compared to Ford and Vauxhall. These problems lay behind BL's decision to abandon the long-standing pattern of piece-work which predominated in the engineering industry, in favour of the time-based system of payment used at both Ford and Vauxhall. In the event the company was not able to prevent the shop floor organization from transforming the new time-based system of measured day-work into a form of effort bargaining as the unions had successfully insisted on the maintenance of 'mutuality' by which changes in working arrangements had to be negotiated (see Chapter 5). The problem was that in order to win acceptance for the shift to time-based payment the management had had to protect current earnings levels which drove a wedge between job times and earnings. The retention of mutuality meant that management had a much harder task subsequently in tightening up job times. It was therefore logical that mutuality should be identified as one of the procedures to be ended when the management introduced its draft agreement, the 'Blue Newspaper', in 1980.

Industrial relations changes

By the 1980s, pay bargaining arrangements were broadly similar between the companies, each having a system of bargaining at the company rather than the plant level, although there were differences in the relative importance of national and lay officials. The biggest changes through the 1970s took place at BL with the centralization of wage bargaining, the process begun with the introduction of measured day-work.

Related moves, pressed for by BL management through the 1970s, included the adoption of a common review date for annual wage agreements; group-wide grade and pay structures, and the adoption of parity between plants; centralized bargaining rather than plant bargaining; and introduction of a group-wide incentive scheme, all of which were finally embodied in the terms of the Blue Newspaper introduced in April, 1980. This trend was accelerated by disputes such as the unsuccessful toolroom workers' strike in 1977 and again in 1979 for separate bargaining arrangements. The Blue Newspaper was not agreed by the unions, although they reluctantly accepted centralized bargaining, and it was implemented by the management on 8 April, 1980.

The Blue Newspaper introduced a number of changes in the procedures for changing working practices, notably mutuality. After the work-force had voted overwhelmingly to accept the company's proposed Recovery Plan on 1 November, 1979, the draft agreement was first presented to the unions and shop stewards. Although it was subsequently rejected in a ballot by the work-force, the main opposition to the changes came from the shop stewards, who saw that they would lead to a major reduction in their bargaining role. After several months of negotiations it was clear to the management that no agreement could be reached, and it was decided to put the changes directly to the work-force. On 25 March, 1980, the company announced that anyone who reported to work on 8 or 9 April would be deemed to have accepted the new conditions laid out in the draft agreement:

'What the stewards called "imposition", and the management called "implementation" went ahead without a major hiccough, and on those two days ... 30 years of management concessions (which had made it impossible to manufacture cars competitively) were thrown out of the window, and our car factories found themselves with a chance of becoming competitive.'   (Edwardes 1983: 135)

Implementation of these changes was seen as central to BL's survival as an independent company given the failure to make substantial productivity gains through the participation scheme introduced in the Ryder period.

The crisis at BL was such that future commercial survival was conditional upon getting the right changes in industrial relations in a fairly short space of time. The situation at Vauxhall, especially in its Ellesmere Port plant, was less dramatic, but the long run of losses meant that in the longer term, the future was no less in doubt.

The reassertion in late 1979 of long-standing written procedure agreements which had been less and less effectively enforced at Vauxhall's Ellesmere Port plant was not really indicative of a long-term industrial relations strategy by the firm. Over the preceding years, the pressure to keep cars flowing on to the market had meant that priority had to be given to buying off any work-force pressure in order to keep production going. As a result, the written agreements were less and less rigorously enforced and shop steward bargaining and custom and practice encroached further into areas of previous managerial prerogative. The opportunity to reassert these agreements, and to drive for greater efficiency arose during the strike of late 1979. During the strike the plant manager set up a small committee to look at ways of increasing the effectiveness within existing agreements, and this culminated in the 'We Will Manage' brief for management. On this occasion, the plant management was perhaps under less pressure to resume production as the domestic market was about to decline quite sharply. The monthly average of new car registrations dropped from 142,000 in 1979 to 127,000 in 1980. The change was perhaps necessary for the continued survival of Vauxhall at Ellesmere Port, but it appears to have been more a case of management seizing an opportunity provided by a long strike to tighten up existing agreements over plant differentials at a time when it was under less pressure to keep its market supplied.

The maintenance of a particular style of industrial relations may be a long-term policy. At Vauxhall, for example, the management's attitude during the current recession has been to let the unions know that it is not pressing its maximum short-term bargaining advantage during a period of high unemployment. The expectation is that the unions would adopt a similarly far-sighted view of their bargaining relation if relative power positions changed.

Although managers think ahead systematically about change in industrial relations practices and procedures, this problem appears to be fairly well downstream in corporate planning. During the 1970s, however, their work in industrial relations had become increasingly one of fire-fighting. Although it had been under discussion for some years, the BL participation scheme was introduced at a time of crisis in 1976, as part of the Ryder strategy, in an effort to give a new legitimacy to management, to gain wider support among the work-force and worker representatives for improvements in performance. It was set up in parallel to normal collective bargaining (and so was never in danger of threatening it) and was oriented primarily to achieving certain changes in organization within the company, and to discussing its model strategy. The Metro was discussed extensively in the participation scheme although the crucial initial planning had taken place before the scheme had been set up.

BL's director of personnel, Pat Lowry, had sought to resolve the company's industrial relations problem in a strategic way and to break away from fire-fighting from dispute to dispute. However his own efforts had become bogged down when Sir Michael Edwardes gave them a new boost. According to Sir Michael, management had compromised so often on general principles in order to resolve individual disputes that the work-force did not take management threats to take a stand on a particular question seriously. For him the watershed came with the 1978 dispute at Bathgate in which it had been necessary to convince the work-force that the company was serious about withdrawing further investment if there were no change in the strike patterns. The outcome of the dispute, as with the closure of Speke, also in 1978, was that 'people were beginning to believe us' (Edwardes 1983: 83). The same might have been said of the situation at Vauxhall's Ellesmere Port plant before the end of 1979.

THE LABOUR MARKET

One general reason why industrial relations and labour management have traditionally been dealt with in a decentralized way in the car industry, as in the engineering as a whole, is that local labour markets have, to a greater or lesser extent, been able to provide employers with a pool of appropriately skilled labour on which they could draw. It has not always been an ideal arrangement because of recurrent problems of skill shortages, but it has provided an alternative to extensive forward planning of labour requirements. Indeed, it has to some extent militated against such action because skilled workers in such a pool can often easily move to another employer without having to undergo much additional training. Local labour market pressures on differentials and on wastage make forward planning difficult.

In theory, and to some extent also in practice, markets can offer a highly decentralized form of decision-making, and the price mechanism provides a decentralized alternative to corporate long-range planning. Traditionally, the longer-range planning has been confined to product development and investment in new equipment, with management relying on local labour markets to provide the required labour at fairly short notice. Under such circumstances, there is little need to plan labour requirements further ahead than the time required for efficient recruitment. These remarks are more true perhaps for BL because of its situation in the heartland of British engineering, but most of the main plants of the other companies are fairly close to major engineering labour markets.

Use of local labour markets may well be inhibited in the future because of the sharp decline in the number of apprentices undergoing training in recent years, and the pressure on major companies to organize their own training schemes for new technology. Thus the potential major skill shortages in the future will place a premium on ways of reducing labour turnover among the skilled labour force. However, in the present adjustments, as shown in Chapter 4, there has so far been no major turning away from local labour markets, although the impact of redundancies and high unemployment has led many employees to favour redeployment and retraining within the same company rather than to look for similar work elsewhere.

CONCLUSIONS

In the late 1970s, the car industry in Britain was being affected by the crisis hitting the European and North American industries and by the extent to which British performance had fallen behind these countries. To varying degrees, all the producers in Britain had to recover this ground as well as respond to the broader crisis posed by the second oil shock, recession, and increased competition from Japan. Although in theory the multinational firms could supply the whole of their British sales from abroad, access to the British car market would become less secure if they did so. British governments would come under stronger pressure to favour the remaining producers in Britain, as might company fleet buyers, who account for about half of the new car purchases.

These difficulties had pushed industrial relations and related labour–management issues into a more central position. As one analyst observed: 'Any firm with confidence in its labour relations would have an immediate cost advantage by the simple expedient of making its standard capacity a larger proportion of the same maximum capacity' (Rhys 1974: 15). But simple as this seems, it does not dictate any particular industrial relations strategy.

Even on a very modest definition of labour relations strategy, such as a set of related policies directed at problems which managements recognize as interrelated, the companies' industrial relations and manpower policies did not always constitute a strategy. Industrial relations objectives were frequently sacrificed in order to meet product market demands. This is not to deny that the companies have long-term objectives in the industrial relations area, but rather that strategy can be overridden by other demands and degenerates into fire-fighting.

The main argument of this chapter has been that the labour management changes which have come about in the industry since the late 1970s have been impelled by the commercial and cost position of all the car producers in the UK. Because the source of inspiration for best practice manufacturing and management methods and of new technology was provided from outside Britain, notably Japan and West Germany, this has led the companies to adopt a broadly similar view of the types of changes to put on their agendas. Thus important themes have been cutting manpower levels down closer to West German and Japanese levels, and the consequent reorganization and change of labour–management policies. Major themes in this have been increased flexibility of deployment of labour, both in terms of moving semi-skilled production workers more easily round the plant, and of changing skill demarcations to enable fewer craftsmen to be employed in any one maintenance job. Technical change has provided an additional impetus for changing skills and job flexibility.

Gaining greater flexibility has an important industrial relations component (highlighted in Chapter 5) because of the need for negotiation. One of the differences between Britain (and to some extent also the USA, where seniority rules in job allocation have been very important) and say West Germany or Japan, has been that even fairly small changes in job descriptions require negotiation between management and shop stewards. Apart from slowing down such changes, this can also increase the cost as management often had to pay a little extra. The most notable examples of this were in the system of 'mutuality' which had prevailed in BL's plants, but such negotiations were not uncommon in the other firms. In comparison, employers in West Germany and especially in Japan had a much freer hand, at least in small day-to-day changes.

Another item on the agenda, inspired partly but not entirely by Japan, was the idea that greater job security for those remaining with the firm after the major employment reductions might be used to encourage greater job flexibility. This philosophy was tried in a limited way in the US car industry negotiations between the UAW and Ford and GM, but could also be found among European producers such as Volvo. This was not a straightforward 'quid pro quo' because greater stability of employment would also enable the companies to invest more in training, and particularly in training their semi-skilled work-force – one of the keys to improved quality of output – as well as to greater flexibility as this requires a broader range of skills.

Organizational change was also on the agenda, in particular as management examined the changes needed in order to follow the Japanese practice of minimizing buffer stocks and improving capital utilization. One of the reasons for high buffer stocks held by the British producers had been to keep production moving despite a large number of unpredictable interruptions occurring both within the factory and among suppliers. Although none of the British producers has adopted the full 'just-in-time' system used in Japan, much attention was devoted to the organizational changes needed to reduce stocks and improve production flow.

To act consistently on these issues demanded a break from the fire-fighting of the 1970s. During the 1970s, although to different degrees, managements had been pushed increasingly away from acting strategically on labour management problems towards fire-fighting. Even the major initiatives, such as BL's participation plan, had an air of crisis about them. One of the roots of fire-fighting in the 1960s and 1970s had been the problem of retaining labour in a buoyant labour market. High rates of labour turnover among certain groups within the labour force (but not all the labour force, for average length of service in the industry is about nine years) may have increased the individual bargaining power of small groups of workers, and this, combined with the overriding objective of getting cars out of the factory gate, pressed management into many concessions of managerial control to the work-force. However, the crisis in the industry in the late 1970s, combined with a steep rise in unemployment, greatly helped management regain the initiative in industrial relations, and to give greater priority to fundamental changes in industrial relations.

Although the car producers in Britain may have had a similar list of possible changes, there have nevertheless been notable differences in approach. Some of these relate to the different positions that each was in at the onset of the crisis of the late 1970s, but others suggest that companies had a degree of choice in labour market strategy.

All four companies have used the change in labour market conditions to reassert management authority, although again they have done so in different ways. Whereas BL has become identified with hard management, especially in its dealings at its Cowley plant, Ford has sought to develop forms of consultation and employee involvement albeit with uneven success. Vauxhall's policy of not pressing for maximum short-term advantage in its dealings with its unions in the expectation that they will behave likewise when conditions are different again illustrates the range of options available.

In the area of job flexibility, again the companies show differences of priority despite being faced by broadly similar problems. BL has so far gone further towards breaking down craft demarcations and obtaining greater flexibility in the use of its craft labour force, but the reason perhaps lies less in the comparative strength or weakness of the unions in the different companies than in how high management puts the question on its bargaining agenda. The immense commercial pressure on BL to maintain its productivity improvements is one reason, but there is also some debate as to how cost effective it is to broaden the range of skills of individual craftsmen. Working practices have perhaps also changed most at BL, enabling the company to claim that its plant at Longbridge has the best productivity level in Europe, which again may indicate a greater priority given by the company to such changes.

One final factor which makes for a degree of similarity of approach to labour management problems between the companies is that they continue to work within the British system of engineering labour markets, which limits their choice in how they organize skilled work. They also continue to work within the British industrial relations environment within a framework of established trade union relations. Unlike the new Nissan plant, all their plants already have fairly long histories, and this in itself limits the degree of change possible and the speed at which it can take place. As mentioned earlier, the continued use of local labour markets for skilled labour means that recruitment decisions can be left well downstream of other commercial decisions both in the sense of the logical order of decisions and of their timing.

THREE
NEW TECHNOLOGY

INTRODUCTION

It is by now commonplace to remark that the rate of innovation in the car industry has become rapid over the last few years. For many, automation in the industry has become synonymous with the use of robotics in assembly operations, and the presumption is that this form of investment will be accompanied by substantial job loss. In part, this relates to an image of work in the industry as being associated with repetitive, short-cycle tasks on a moving assembly line which are extremely vulnerable to the application of automated techniques.

However, it is important to remember first, that the production process in car manufacture involves several distinct stages; second, that these stages have been unevenly affected by technical change; third, that car manufacturing typically experiences process innovations such as robotic assembly in tandem with the development of new products; and fourth, that robotic assembly affects only some of the production stages, and to a different extent. This chapter looks at the precise nature and extent of the technical changes which have occurred in the UK, and their implications for industrial relations. In addition, we shall look at the evidence which suggests that the latest spate of innovations has fundamentally affected economies of scale within the industry; if it is correct to say that minimum efficient scale economies in production have been reduced by the increasing flexibility of capital equipment,[1] then this has implications not only for the survival of Austin Rover (the volume car division of BL) as a medium-sized producer, but also for labour relations in the UK where, for example, strike proneness is related to the failure to achieve minimum efficient scale (Jones and Prais 1978). At the outset, it is useful to consider the nature of the manufacturing process itself.

THE MANUFACTURING PROCESS[2]

Figure 1 outlines the basic sequence of operations in car manufacture: for the moment, we shall leave design consider-ations aside. Beginning with the raw material suppliers, two sets of operations proceed. The first has to do with the production of the 'power-train' (essentially the engine, trans-mission, and axles) which are first cast or forged then subsequently machined and assembled. The second results in the production of a welded, painted car body: initially, sheet metal is stamped to produce panels in a press shop; these are welded to form sub-assemblies and then a rigid body in the body shop. Finally, paint is applied. The results of these two sets of operations are married during the final assembly operation, when the thousands of components which constitute 'trim' are fitted.

These operations do not normally occur on the same site: they need not even all occur within the same company. Currently, in Austin Rover panel pressing occurs at Swindon as well as at Cowley. Power-train production and body assembly both take place on the Longbridge site, but engines are shipped from Longbridge to Cowley. Within Ford, Dagenham has been the most integrated UK site for some time, covering all operations until the closure of the foundry this year. However, Halewood receives material from Dagenham, and Escort engines are manufactured at Bridgend. In the UK, Vauxhall and Talbot are mainly concerned with the assembly of kits.

The firms also differ in the extent to which they undertake all the manufacturing operations themselves. All major car firms make at least some of their own engines and gearboxes

Figure 1 Automobile production – sequence of operations

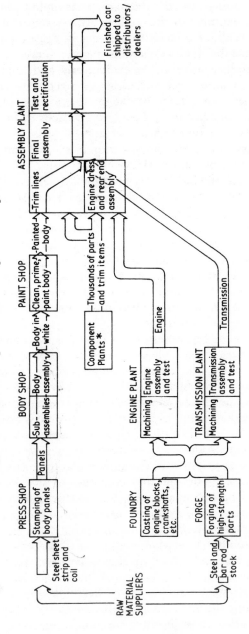

* Internal and outside sources of supply

Source: CPRS 1975: 13.

as well as doing all of their own assembly. However, collaborative ventures in this area imply out-sourcing: Austin Rover make bodies for Rolls Royce cars, and use power-train elements made by both Volkswagen and Honda. Ford has tended to produce more of its components and intermediate inputs such as mild steel and glass but even here there are differences between phases of the production process, with many trim components being bought in. Moreover, for reasons we shall discuss below, vertical integration of activities is no longer practised by all the major companies: Ford will now no longer make castings in the UK, while for some time Peugeot engines powered the Sierra diesel option.[3]

Dispersal of activity may occur for a number of reasons. For example, Halewood may be seen as the last survivor of the attempt to change the pattern of industrial location initiated by government regional policies in the 1960s, which at one stage promoted car assembly activity in Liverpool as well as in Scotland. Another might be the concern to avoid large concentrations of employees, owing to the greater strike proneness of larger plants in Britain as compared with other countries (Jones and Prais 1978).

Table 4 presents several estimates of scale economies drawn together by Owen (1983). These pre-date the impact of robotics in body assembly. The estimates do vary, but a number of points emerge. The first is that there are obvious advantages to using the same engine and transmission combination across a range of models and because of the capital costs of die changes similar considerations apply to body panels. The problem for car producers is, as Rhys (1974) notes of British Leyland in the 1970s, how to design and market a model range so as to achieve model-specific economies of scale while not sacrificing the marketing advantages of product differentiation.

Finally, although car production did undergo radical changes in the 1970s these affected the various parts of the production process differently.[4] In stamping, the use of larger and faster presses, of pick and place machines between presses and automated loading and die change had simultaneously reduced manning requirements and increased flexibility since the early 1950s. At about the same time, the UK industry had invested in first-generation transfer lines in engine machining areas

Table 4 *Estimates of minimum efficient scales (ooo units p.a.)*

source of estimates	foundry and forge	operations		
		pressing	engine and transmission	final assembly
Pratten[a]	1,000	500	250	300
Rhys[b]	200	2,000	1,000	200
White[c]	'small'	400	260	200
Ford UK[d]	2,000			300
McGee[e]		2,000		
Euro-Economics[f]	2,000	2,000	1,000	250

Source: Owen 1983.

a C. F. Pratten, *Economies of Scale in Manufacturing Industry* (Cambridge, 1971).

b D. G. Rhys, *The Motor Industry: An Economic Survey* (London, 1972).

c L. J. White, *The Automobile Industry Since 1945* (Cambridge, Mass., 1971).

d Evidence to the House of Commons Expenditure Committee Session 1974–75, Minutes of Evidence taken before the Trade and Industry Sub-Committee, Vol. I.

e John S. McGee, 'Economies of Size in Auto Body Manufacture', *Journal of Law and Economics*, Vol. XVI (2), October, 1973.

f *Euro-Economics*, 'The European Car Industry – The Problem of Structure and Overcapacity', March, 1975.

(Bloomfield 1978: 43; Maxcy and Silbertson 1959: 58–9). However, in the early 1970s, despite the use of a certain number of multiwelders and power tools, the assembly operations – engine assembly, body assembly, and trim and final assembly – remained labour intensive. The moving assembly track, introduced into the UK in final assembly in the 1920s, and body assembly in the 1930s, remained substantially unchanged until the 1970s.

Assembly areas accounted for the greater proportion of labour costs (*Table 5*). Approximately half the total labour input occurred in body and final assembly and within power-train production, engine assembly represented the largest element of labour cost. There existed substantial scope for the

Table 5 *Distribution of labour input*

operation	percentage of total labour hours
panel production	10
body assembly	30
power-train production	25
paint	10
trim and final assembly	20
inspection, etc.	5
total	100

Source: Derived from CPRS 1975: 14–16.

application of microprocessor-based process innovation to reduce labour costs in the industry. However, reduction in labour costs was not the only purpose of technical change: in order to understand the attractions of new technology for the industry in the 1970s one needs to look at the overall pattern of product and process change.

PROCESS AND PRODUCT INNOVATION

The most systematic attempt to explain the pattern of change in the industry is that of Abernathy (1978) who extends theories about the product life cycle to explain the parallel pattern of process change. His model suggests that the early phase of the industry is characterized by relatively fluid, inefficient production processes, and a high level of product differentiation and change. Subsequently a dominant standard product design emerges, which is produced at high volume and achieves substantial market success. This success encourages the development of mass production techniques with very high process efficiency, but as a consequence further radical product innovation is rendered difficult because it requires scrapping of expensive capital equipment. However, this stable condition cannot survive indefinitely, and factors such as technical change or a radical shift in market tastes induce a period of uncertainty, characterized by renewed product innovation and the entry into the market of new firms competing on product quality and performance as well as price. However, such product differentiation occurs within the constraints of scale economies, and these are achieved through varying combinations of common basic components (Abernathy, Clark, and Kantrow 1983).

Thus there is a dynamic link between innovations in products and the production process; there is a trade-off between, first, standardization and high productivity; second, the capacity of manufacturers to accommodate radical change; and third, the ability of the industry to adapt to sudden change. This implies the avoidance of overwhelming reliance on dedicated capital equipment, a concern with both price and non-price competition, and the avoidance of backward integration of all stages of the production process. The world car industry is seen to have experienced two phases of 'de-maturity'. The first, following the general adoption of the all-steel car body in the 1920s was characterized by the failure of Ford's one-model low-price strategy based on the Model T. Faced with competition from the new, differentiated GM model range, Ford had to close down a rigid but efficient production system to retool for a new, more marketable model and never recovered market leadership. The second phase of 'dematurity', marked by a period of product and process innovation, followed from the arrival of Japanese competition on the world scene during a period of rapid inflation in the price of oil.

The causes of these changes are more varied than those Abernathy discusses. From outside the industry legislative standards on safety and emission control have, particularly in the USA, demanded changes as has the rapidly falling cost of information processing technology. Nevertheless, product innovation is probably the more important catalyst for change. This is because particular process changes are deployed as part of a competitive strategy in which the development of a marketable product range is of primary importance: quality improvement and superior performance are more important than marginal price differences. It is best, therefore, to discuss product changes first.

These may be broadly divided into those which increase the power gained from a given amount of fuel and those which decrease body weight and resistance (OECD 1983: 56). The first set includes changes to petrol engines, such as improved compression ratios and combustion, as well as the development of diesel engines and of variable-speed transmissions. The second set includes changes to the design and aerodynamics of the car body, and the increased use of plastics and electronics, the latter both in instrumentation and ignition control.[5]

The implications of such innovations for process change differ substantially. Improvements to engine compression could be effected by machining on existing transfer lines, while the increase in the use of in-car electronics is likely to result in a higher percentage of components bought in rather than process changes within the car companies themselves. The introduction of diesel engine manufacture or new transmission designs require substantial change, but new body assembly techniques have brought about the most radical process changes of the last decade. In general terms, though, the link between product and process change is close, whether the concern is with quality or costs. For example, reduced air resistance and a lighter and more watertight car body are much easier to achieve with more reliable automated welding.

The importance of the microprocessor-based changes introduced over the last decade has been fundamental. Robotics applications affect stamping, engine, body, and final assembly. Computer numerical control affects engine and transmission machining. Computer-aided design reduces design overheads and lead times as well as opening up the possibility of computer-aided engineering, reducing demand for skilled tool-room labour. Substantial process efficiency improvements are possible using computer-aided modelling of production flow, automated inspection, computerized scheduling, and stock control.

It is argued by some that the flexibility inherent in this generation of changes can affect economies of scale in the industry by reducing the capital costs of model change (Altshuler et al. 1984). Given the capabilities of flexible manufacturing systems, capital costs may be spread over several models or indeed several generations of models. The results may be substantial. The OECD (1983) suggests that minimum efficient scale for an assembly plant may have been reduced from 400,000 to 250,000 units per year, and that the break-even points of the US producers may have fallen substantially. For example, that GM may have been reduced by anything from 4 to 8 million units per annum and for Ford from 4.2 million to 3 million units (OECD 1983: 97). Moreover, such global figures may disguise a more highly differentiated product. Although this generation of changes would not remove the need for a common base of standardized components within a model range, and although scale economies in certain areas such as final assembly need not change, there may be a tendency towards the production of a larger range of units, each at lower volumes, on a given line.

There may be a number of problems with this argument as applied to the UK industry. First, the innovations to the manufacturing systems have not in practice led to the levels of flexibility suggested. Second, although the equipment in engine machining or body assembly areas may be able to deal with several products, doubts remain about the lifespan of the equipment and product ranges as well as the marketability of highly differentiated products at one point in time. Third, despite advances in design technology, there remain considerable design costs attached to the development of new models and, as Abernathy (1978) has shown, at least up to 1973 the returns to model change were quite low. New market conditions may improve the returns to such change, but it is still by no means certain that market demand will encourage full use of the technical potential of such equipment.

Nevertheless, a reduction in minimum efficient scale for a model range would assist the medium-sized producers, particularly BL. This can be illustrated by *Figure* 2, which shows Pratten's cost calculations for the industry in 1971 adjusted to take account of the technical changes discussed here. Curve SS shows the break-even cost/volume relationship for BL beforehand and curve S'S' shows the effect of the changes. At 1982 output, this would have reduced the BL cost index by 5 per cent. Put another way, BL could have retained the same unit costs producing 140,000 less vehicles per year.

However it is important to note that there is a range of technical options available to manufacturers within each stage of the production process and that selection is made on the basis of individual manufacturing needs. As we noted above,

Figure 2 Cost/volume relationships

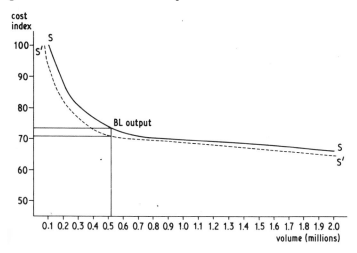

these can differ in several important respects such as volume, model range, and sourcing patterns. Thus to take a simple example, while some firms have invested extensively in robots in the welding process, others continue to use multiwelders which do not have the same flexibility. This is partly because new investment is not made for its own sake but on the basis of its contribution to the cost effectiveness and quality of manufacturing the product and also because, once installed, capital equipment is expected to work over a number of years to repay the investment; so, decisions on capital investment are likely to have long-term repercussions. For these reasons and because the rate of innovation remains rapid, the differences between manufacturers in their use of new technologies are likely to remain pronounced. As the next section will show, even within the UK different options in use of automated equipment have emerged.

DEVELOPMENTS IN THE UK[6]

The British car industry undertook large-scale automation later than a number of overseas competitors. Although robots were used by Volkswagen, Fiat, Renault, and Saab in the early 1970s, automated welding first appeared on a large scale in the UK in 1976 on the Ford Fiesta line. At BL change came later, the first large-scale use of robotics and multiwelders in body assembly being on the Metro line at Longbridge and despite the earlier changes at Ford it is reasonable to identify the Metro line as the first to be extensively automated.

Such was the magnitude of this innovation that the Metro line at Longbridge had more money spent on it than the total spent at Cowley for both Maestro and Montego. Much of the £275 million spent on Metro production went on the new West Works body plant. Throughout the planning for the Metro production, managers were primarily concerned to get tried and tested systems rather than absolute state-of-the-art technology, in order to be sure that the planned production runs would be achieved. This meant that some manual operations were initially retained, as for example the carbon dioxide welding on underframe assemblies. Similarly, inflexible multiwelders were preferred to flexible robotic systems, and programmable logic controllers (PLCs) were used to locate and diagnose breakdowns.

Metro body components are not built at Longbridge, but brought in from Llanelli and Swindon, two of the old Pressed Steel Fisher plants. Again the partial degree of technical innovation favoured by BL for this project was exemplified in the body building process. The press lines which build the subframes and their components were highly automated, one line requiring one press mechanic and two more operators to remove the finished components. On the other hand, the next stages of sub-frame construction involving the assembly and weld of the various parts were performed manually, a carousel arrangement being used to sequence the tack welding, spot welding, and carbon dioxide welding on the various jigs. The subsequent drilling and reaming processes were also designed to incorporate a mixture of automated and manual operations, and transfer and inspection of the assemblies to the paint line was also performed manually. More recent process innovations at Cowley have now enabled these tasks to be automated.

At the other main Austin Rover assembly plant, Cowley, the Maestro and Montego are produced. To an extent the production lines for these two models are integrated and there is a significant area of commonality of parts in both the body and power-train, but this is not a new production strategy. To obtain the economies of scale of engine production, duplication through a range of models and over a series of cars has been the norm. Indeed the 'A plus' engine used in some versions of the Metro, Maestro, and Montego is a derivative of a pre-war 'A' series engine developed by Austin.

However the use of computer-aided design and manufacturing (CAD/CAM) for body and engine development is new. These techniques do away with the need for the making and remaking of drawings, for example in the preparation of dies. So the Montego design was initiated from the existing Maestro database held on computer for transmission to VDU when necessary. In this way about 60 per cent of the Maestro's body panels were utilized on the Montego. Similarly the new 'S' series engine developed for the Montego was designed from the Maestro's 'R' series, subsequently replacing it on both models. The speed of this innovation was in itself unprecedented but has been rendered technically possible and economically feasible by computerized engineering. CAD was used, for example, to determine the optimum wall thickness of the new cylinder block, and to provide information for manufacture of casting patterns which will remain consistent throughout the production life of the engine. The advantages of computerized techniques are clearly demonstrated here. Pre-production and test, the conception and execution of manufacture including the prototype stages are now integrated rather than being segmented phases. Repeated experimentation in the design of body shape or individual components becomes possible without the need for a series of prototype builds until final specifications are established.

In practice computer-aided engineering (CAE) is applied in a piecemeal way. One example was its use in redesigning the Land Rover chassis for new models, to adapt it for changing patterns of demand and the greater tendency for its use on roads. The design problem centred on reconciling this with the continuing need for strength and flexibility for use off roads and was resolved through a five-stage design and test programme. CAE was also used to explore the implications of using different types of material in design of body panels in terms of cost, strength, and mass.

Its claimed advantages are therefore the flexibility it permits in design, the precision it provides for high automation of the manufacturing process (particularly the numerical control techniques of machine tool manufacture), a more comprehensive product development system which ensures greater quality, as, for example, in the dimensions of the body panels, and the reduced lead times required to introduce new products.

All car manufacturers are using CAE, but Austin Rover is distinct in the degree of automation it has pursued on the production line. Cowley receives body pressings from the Swindon facility and from various non-BL suppliers. These are then welded to form the various sub-assemblies. Until 1984 both front and rear underframes were welded manually in jigs, but these operations have now been replaced by multiwelders. As cars are built from the floor upwards the underframes are assembled first. Robots and multiwelders are used, the distinction between the two being that robots are capable of movement through their working arms, and may be programmed to deal with a variety of tasks, in this instance frame shapes. Hence variations between the Montego and Maestro may be accommodated within one line, a feature that was not developed to the same extent when the Metro line was installed because that used more multiwelders. Matching of panels is automatically controlled for the finish welding, and an indication of the speed of production is illustrated by the completion of 184 welds in less than 60 seconds. Side panels are similarly welded by a combination of multiwelders and robots.

Here the line splits for the body framing, or the joining of the various parts of the car frame into one unit. Again this is an automated process, and one which has been so for some years; but it is an area in which Austin Rover claims greater flexibility has been developed in that the machines can now identify and weld up to five body variants in any order within each model. This is possible because each station has a tool change facility which can be executed within the individual job cycle time enabling maximum capacity utilization of plant, so that the line is (theoretically) producing vehicles all the time.

The second area of production which approaches complete automation is in the paint shop. Reporting ten years ago, the Central Policy Review Staff noted that one of the objectives of automation in this area was to achieve a satisfactory quality level.

> 'Most modern plants have automatic precleaning and priming lines and automatic spray booths, at least for the initial enamel coat.... While the labour content is relatively small (less than 10% of total labour), the skill required in painting is substantial. Customers are more critical of paint finish than almost any other aspect of car quality.'   (1975: 15)

Quality is thus seen as an important advantage of increased automation. Others include the speed of throughput – at Cowley seventy-two vehicles an hour can be processed through priming, pre-treatment, paint sealer, and waxing – and the reduction in safety hazards. The gradual nature of progress in automating this area mainly related to designing sufficiently manoeuvrable robots, and in the view of one study this represents one major limitation to the rate of diffusion of robots (West Midlands County Council, Sector Report No. 5, 1984). It is also significant that technical innovation has been accompanied by reforms to work organization. Cowley management have claimed increases in 'right first time' output to match any European rival, yet it is acknowledged that this is not only due to new technology but also to 'good working practices'.

Although trim and final assembly are not as highly automated, several innovations point to future changes. Automatic transfer lines have been augmented by conveyors which store and select painted bodies as well as co-ordinating the arrival of components at the track side, a crucial factor in efficient capacity utilization and minimizing stockholding. The 'sniffer robot' introduced on the Triumph Acclaim line in 1981 has been extended to Maestro/Montego production, and is also used at Longbridge. This device checks for waterproofing and the fit of the panels by pressurizing the cabin with helium and then testing for leakages. Previously hundreds of gallons of water would have been sprayed to detect leaks, and could often cause damage to internal trim.

One of the latest innovations in robot technology operates on the Montego line, fitting windscreens and rear windows. The technical advances relate to the robot's ability to work on a moving assembly line and to marry the screen to the body accurately (within one millimetre tolerance). This is done by using four cameras which locate the body as it moves along the assembly line. Such sophisticated equipment was expensive to develop and was said to cost £900,000 as a finished unit. Auto-glazing makes little saving in terms of labour, but, from management's point of view, its advantage lies in product quality, and for that reason its use will be extended to the Maestro and Rover XX project in the future.

This concern with quality is a crucial indicator of where management thinking on technical innovation in BL is heading. To quote the Managing Director (Operations) of ARG: 'Every new robot must be justified on the basis of increased efficiency and an enhanced level of consistently high quality. That is why we are deliberately introducing robots in the trim and final assembly area for example, on quality sensitive operations such as screen fitment.' (*Automobile Engineer*, April/May, 1984, p. 56)

At Ford, technical innovation has also been geared to new product introduction. Like ARG it has concentrated on the body shell and paint areas, using automation to improve quality and raise productivity both through raised output and by reducing sub-standard work. Thus at Halewood, where the Escort and Orion models are built, Ford had a substantial number of different types of robots installed by 1980 for welding the floor pan, engine compartment, and side panels. Transference between stages is also performed by robot. Automation was seen as crucial because of the improved accuracy. The resulting greater torsional strength could then be translated into lighter body materials to improve fuel economy; automation has allowed up to a 15 per cent reduction in the number of welds without sacrificing body strength.

Ford also claim improvements to work standards and organization through automation. Replacing the old system of carousels which each had sixteen jigs, used on the Escort Mark I, removed an area of work where the short task cycle times had, in the past, created friction in industrial relations and also made maintenance difficult. In addition, Ford has automated the body shell manufacture and the painting process at Halewood. It is accepted, however, that automation can create problems, particularly with breakdowns, so self-diagnosis has become more important for repair and maintenance. Despite the size of investment involved, it is notable that Ford duplicates its innovation at Saarlouis, the other Escort plant for European markets, one major advantage of this being that by exchanging information on all job specifications and cycle times the company ensures that manufacturing techniques are consistently being upgraded.

One result of this upgrading was the further innovation for the introduction of the Orion in 1983. In total £18 million was spent, much of it on new handling systems and more spot welding robots as well as a new paint system. Given the degree of commonality between body and floor pans between the Escort and Orion models some integration in production is possible, but as yet Ford has not opted for the degree of flexible manufacturing achieved by BL at Cowley. However at Dagenham where the Fiesta and Sierra are assembled considerable flexibility has been achieved, with robots being able to handle a sequence of different models and body types for both models on the finish welding process using 24 Cincinnatti Millicron robots. This is one result of the £500 million spent on process development for the Sierra and retooling for the 'reskinned' Fiesta. The high levels of automation are indicated by the fact that 88 per cent of all spot welding is carried out automatically, and that the Sierra requires only 503 manual welds while its predecessor, the Cortina, had 3,508. One result is the single side outer panel used on the Sierra in replacement for the eight panels used on the Cortina, despite the fact that the former is a much larger car. Besides the cost factors, other objectives of these changes were fuel economies with sustained performance and the quality of fit of the different parts of the body.

Many elements of the Sierra power-train resemble its predecessor, the Cortina. The engines remain essentially unchanged, for example, although modifications to the final drive casing were perfected using laser holography and finite element modelling. However Ford has changed its engine manufacturing policy and petrol engine production is now concentrated in Germany, while Dagenham has become the centre of diesel engine production for Ford Europe. The high degree of automation of the new engine line at Dagenham indicates that, like BL, the company is committed to extending automation beyond the body and paint shops. But it must be emphasized that automation is not undertaken purely to displace labour. Certainly in some areas the need to raise productivity has been a prime motivating factor under pressure from persistently intense competition. Other factors are also germane though, in particular the need to sustain high product quality and reliability, a central feature of the car market being customer satisfaction with these points. The need for consistently high plant utilization to secure economies of scale is another. Third, as a capital investment robots can be costed more precisely than labour, assisting budgeting forecasts.[7]

It is difficult to predict where the limits to automation lie. The changes introduced by Vauxhall Ellesmere Port for the revised Astra in 1984 are, for example, very similar to those made by ARG and Ford. They are concentrated in the body assembly area where a mixture of multiwelders and robots perform welding tasks, and in the paint shop where further automation has taken place. At Talbot investment has also been principally to modernize the paint shop facilities. Moreover, automation of body welding and the paint process has not been limited to the mass producers and even specialist firms like Jaguar and Land Rover have invested in new manufacturing processes. When transferring production to its new Solihull plant, Land Rover introduced an automated engine line, for example, and where sixty-five men were previously employed there are now thirteen. Yet one study has suggested that Austin Rover has reached its quota of robots for existing lines, at least at Longbridge (WMCC 1984: 85). This seems correct in so far as we have seen that process innovation is closely linked to new products; but as product innovation becomes more central to the nature of competition between the world's car manufacturers, so we may expect investment in new technologies to be sustained.

To summarize the arguments presented so far:

1. The process of technological change has accelerated rapidly under pressure of oil prices and increasing competition, particularly from Japanese producers. It has also been facilitated by microelectronic developments.

2. Process innovation has been concentrated upon the body shop and in the painting process. Robot welders and automatic conveyance of parts have been major changes. Robot sprayers have also been introduced.

3. Computer-aided engineering has changed product innovation and process development. This now constitutes an integrated system of development design and test to the production stage. Numerical control of manufacturing standards enables tools and equipment to be developed from computerized data. Substantial economies are said to stem from this.

4. Managers have indicated their intention to move to robot production in other areas of manufacturing. BL have in particular stressed the importance of automating power-train and final assembly as a means of achieving Japanese standards: 'It is by investing in this way that we will begin to approach Japanese manufacturing in terms of productivity and come close to matching their pace of new product innovation.'[7]

5. Process and product innovation are interlinked. In the past, general retooling of a plant has taken place every thirty years or so; Ford's Dagenham plant was opened in the 1930s, renovated in 1959, and retooled again in 1980–82. Alongside these major changes, smaller innovations are continuously being made however.

6. A key objective of the most recent wave of process innovation is manufacturing flexibility. Such flexibility is one element of the shift in the technical economies of scale: this is particularly important for Austin Rover. Because of the European basis of their production, Ford have not thus far attempted to introduce flexible manufacturing to such an extent. The events described here thus broadly support the argument summarized in *Figure 1* that Austin Rover in particular is of such a size that small shifts in volume of output may have substantial repercussions on unit costs. We shall return to this point below.

CONCLUSIONS

The discussion of technical change in the motor industry relates directly to the argument of the previous one, for it is product market and customer pressures which encourage product change and this in turn encourages process innovation intended either to reduce costs or to improve quality.[8] Every major manufacturer has introduced new technology based on microelectronic applications but thus far the automation of the manufacturing process has concentrated on two stages in particular. These are the body construction stage where multiwelders and robots are used for welding, and in the paint process where robot sprayers are also used. The use of advanced technology at the body assembly stage has three sets of consequences. The first is labour displacement; for example, Willman and Winch (1985) calculate reductions of up to 80 per cent in certain areas of the Longbridge plant. However, the implications of change extend beyond the stage of production directly affected and the second consequence is a renewed pressure for improved process efficiency in other linked areas of production. For although the productive capacity of automated body assembly techniques tends to be much greater than manual techniques, such gains may be lost if downstream activities remain inefficient. This is particularly true of the labour intensive final assembly area. Yet where the prime concern is to improve productivity, technical change at any stage of the production process represents only one element of a broad strategy (*Figure 3*).

The third set of consequences concern scale economies and volumes. If flexibility in manufacturing allows a wider model range to be produced at lower volumes on any model, then the close relationship of process and product innovation may alter in the future. Not only may plants be less vulnerable to short-term fluctuations in demand for a given model but in the longer term process innovation may be incremental rather than episodic. Such changes may affect patterns of employment and bargaining at company and plant level.

Overall, these technological changes affect four areas of interest for industrial relations. The increasing use of electronics and the decrease in direct labour requirements implies that

Figure 3 Components of standard and off standard hours

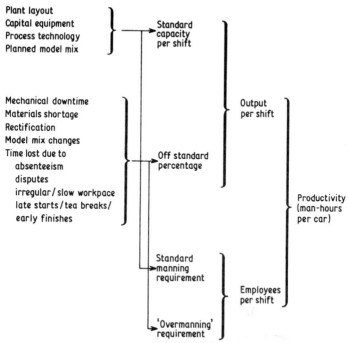

Source: derived from Hartley (1981), *Figure 4.2*

there may be a change in the pattern of demand for skills in the industry as a whole. The emphasis on improved process efficiency and the altered pattern of product and process innovation imply in turn changes to the pattern of labour utilization and deployment and thus to working practices in the industry. Furthermore, these factors imply a changing pattern of strike activity. On the one hand, given that new technology implies alterations to employment levels and job content, the process of introducing this may provoke conflict. On the other hand, innovation promises to alter production scales and the response of the firms to product market fluctuations, both factors which have tended to influence the pattern of strikes in the car industry in the past. Finally, trade union organization and behaviour may be influenced by organizational changes and by employment changes induced by innovation.

In the four chapters that follow, we shall look at skills, working practices, strike activity, and union strategies in the light of the changes outlined here and in the previous chapter.

FOUR
SKILLS, TRAINING, AND INTERNAL LABOUR MARKETS

INTRODUCTION

The drive for increased productivity and technical changes in the British car industry has led to a major reduction in manpower and a number of important changes in the mix of occupations. This chapter examines some of these changes, and compares their impact in Britain with that in other countries. It also looks at changes in skill requirements and training, and whether these have brought about a change in the relationship between the companies and their local labour markets.

The extent of technical changes and of changes in working practices can affect the relationship between the car companies and their local labour markets. In a number of the other European countries and in the USA there has been something of a turning away from use of local labour markets as a prime source of new labour, and as a source of flexibility. Particularly in West Germany and Sweden, but also in the USA, a number of car companies appear to have placed a greater emphasis upon adjustment of their labour forces by retraining and redeployment between functions in the place of the traditional image of an industry which took on and laid off labour as the market successively expanded and contracted. This has arisen partly from the belief that increased security of employment may be an acceptable quid pro quo for the acceptance of greater flexibility of deployment by the labour force. It has also arisen from the increased awareness of the employment practices of the large Japanese companies which offer their core labour force the prospect of long-term employment, but expect in return that their employees should accept retraining and internal redeployment. In Britain, extensive use of internal redeployment of labour could transform the organization of British labour markets. These depend upon a large number of different employers using identical job categories are traditionally organized on an occupational basis. Indeed, these occupations are further protected by the trade union practice of job demarcation rules.

One convenient shorthand expression which should be introduced at this point is the term 'internal labour market'. This is best explained by considering an employer's choice in filling a particular vacancy as one between looking outside the firm to its local labour market, and looking for a suitable internal candidate to fill the job, looking to the firm's 'internal labour market'. The term will thus be used to describe the set of employment practices in which companies look to their existing employees as the prime source for filling certain vacancies. Under such conditions, the vacancies communicated to the local labour market may be for trainee positions, or other types of entry grade. The internal labour markets of the large Japanese firms provide one example in which skilled labour is almost entirely recruited from among school leavers, with people being trained and promoted internally rather than recruited into skilled positions directly from outside. One advantage to employers is that such skills may be more closely tailored to their individual needs. But the disadvantage is that such skills are not easily transferable between employers so that lay-offs are likely to be strongly resisted by employees, and employers cannot quickly expand their skilled labour force by direct recruitment from outside.

The high levels of efficiency of Japanese car producers can in part be attributed to their pattern of internal labour markets with their absence of rigid job demarcations, and the flexibility of deployment of their labour forces. However, employers are not always able to take advantage of such potential internal flexibility. In the US car industry, for example, redeployment of labour within the firm has been until recently greatly restricted by the system of seniority rules which had been negotiated to regulate upgrading and the order in which workers are to be laid off and re-engaged. Seniority rules applied only within certain groups of jobs, seniority districts, and could often not be carried over to other jobs. A number of the studies in the 'Future of the Automobile' project have suggested that employers in West Germany, Sweden, and to some extent also the USA have been pursuing a policy of cultivating their internal labour markets, and of reducing their traditional reliance upon local labour markets both as a source of skilled manpower, and as a means of adjustment to product market fluctuations. In the USA and France, where such internal labour markets already existed, employers have sought to make them more flexible. This chapter looks at some of these developments, and considers whether there are parallels in the British car industry. It also examines the nature of the manpower changes in the industry in recent years, and asks how far these have affected company manpower policies. It looks first at the recent manpower reductions in the context of past employment fluctuations in the industry, and then at their influence upon the structure of the industry's labour force. It then will look more specifically at the changes in practices of the individual companies.

LABOUR FORCE REDUCTIONS

The car industry in Britain has faced a strongly fluctuating market throughout the post-war period. On the whole, year-to-year fluctuations in employment in the industry have varied mostly between plus or minus 5 per cent. But on four separate occasions, in response to sales, output of domestically produced cars and vans fell by between 10 per cent and 20 per cent from one year to the next, in 1955–56, 1960–61, 1974–75, and 1980–81. There were also a number of equally dramatic increases in sales, often associated with pre-election booms, as is illustrated in *Figure 4*.[1] These bigger year-to-year changes in the industry's product demand led to large variations in its labour require-ments. To cope with such fluctuations, the industry has relied heavily upon its ability to attract labour in times of boom, and to lay it off in times of recession. Thus the industry's reputation

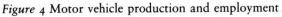

Figure 4 Motor vehicle production and employment

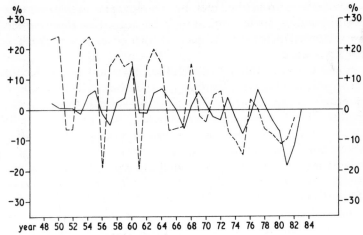

Source: Economic Trends, DE Gazette.

for 'hire and fire'. The companies have borne some of the burden of these fluctuations by laying people off less than proportionately to falls in output, and they have tended to do so after a lag, and similarly, when output was rising they recruited less than proportionately. This has two consequences. First, although fluctuations in pay and overtime absorbed part of the demand fluctuations, the companies have also borne part of the cost. Second, car demand often fell just as manpower levels appeared to reach their newly planned level, leaving the companies with a large surplus of labour over their immediate short-run needs. This put heavy pressure on the production standards set by industrial engineers, and was no doubt one of the sources of slippage in productivity levels discussed in the next chapter.

According to Jones and Prais (1978) such output fluctuations have been a feature of the industry in other countries also, yet they have not affected employment levels. According to Streeck and Hoff (1983) during the 1970s employment changes followed output fluctuations most closely in the USA, Japan, and Britain; less so in West Germany and France; and hardly at all in Italy and Sweden.[2] In the USA this was facilitated by lay-off agreements, and in Japan by a large secondary labour force not benefiting from the 'lifetime' employment system and by subcontracting. In Britain, as will be argued in this chapter, the relationship between firms and their local labour markets is a key factor.

Employment in the industry did not start its current decline until 1978, and between March 1978 and March 1983 it declined by nearly 40 per cent from its peak of 485,000 to just under 300,000 (Department of Employment, SIC 1968: 381). The figures for the individual car companies were as follows: BL's labour force declined by 67 per cent from 147,000 in 1979 to only 80,000 by 1983; Ford's declined by 16 per cent from 80,000 in 1979 to 64,000 in 1983, with a further 4,000 job losses planned for 1983–86; and Vauxhall's dropped by 36 per cent from 33,000 in 1979 to 21,000 in 1983. Employment at Talbot declined from 24,000 in 1979 to 7,000 in 1983, including the closure of its Linwood plant in 1981, and reductions at its Ryton assembly and Stoke engine plants (Jones 1985).

Despite reductions of such scale, Ford has used no compulsory redundancies, nor has Vauxhall apart from one small group of about sixty. These companies have relied mostly upon a mixture of early retirements, voluntary redundancies, and natural wastage combined with reduced recruitment, although the efficacy of the latter usually declines in recession. A similar picture could be found at BL and Talbot except that there were a number of major plant closures.

It may seem paradoxical that in a period of high unemployment so many people should be prepared to volunteer for redundancy. Indeed, in their second round of job losses in 1983, Ford had more volunteers than the number sought, and was able to use this as a bargaining counter to achieve changes in individual jobs.

A number of factors may help to explain the success of voluntary redundancies especially when closure is not likely. First, the terms offered by the company have to be perceived as reasonable. In the redundancy plans announced at Ford in 1983 at its Halewood plant, for example, payments for voluntary redundancy for a grade C assembly worker ranged from £2,900 for someone aged 25 with 5 years' service to £6,300 for a person aged 45 with 20 years' service. For early retirement, a person of 55 with 20 years' pensionable service could expect £7,000, equivalent to almost one year's gross earnings. These were considerably above the legally prescribed minima.

Second, the alternatives open to people facing possible redundancy can affect their behaviour. In the industry as a whole in both 1980 and 1981 there was extensive short-time working. According to the Department of Employment in 1980 and 1981 respectively 6.2 per cent and 12.4 per cent of operatives were losing a weekly average of 13.5 and 12.7 hours through short-time. In addition, the percentage of operatives working overtime had dropped from about 40 per cent to 27 per cent and then to 20 per cent. The car industry itself made extensive use of short-time working in this period, using the government's Temporary Short-Time Working Compensation Scheme under which employers would keep workers on short-time instead of making them redundant, and receive compensation from the government. The consequent drop in weekly earnings caused many workers to put pressure on their union negotiators to settle redundancy terms quickly to get back to normal working and normal earnings levels. It would also induce a number of more mobile workers to look for higher earnings elsewhere, perhaps to beat the rush for jobs after the redundancies had been agreed.

One additional factor, which may help to explain why managements often found it was easier to obtain redundancies in Britain than it was for their continental European counterparts may lie in the organization of British labour markets. This point will be taken up later, but two observations should be made here. First, a system of well-developed local labour markets for engineering skills such as exists in the West Midlands, and also now in the London area, means that many workers expect to be able to find similar jobs requiring their skills in other firms. Despite the very high levels of unemployment, and the increased number of people unemployed for over twelve months, the flows on to and off the unemployment register over a year are considerably greater than the number of unemployed at any time. While many workers may have friends experiencing difficulty finding work, they are also likely to have other friends who leave jobs and are successful in finding new ones. Moreover, in 1980, the year of most severe job losses in the industry started, the June unemployment rates were considerably lower than now: in Oxfordshire 4.7 per cent, in Essex 5.8 per cent, in Luton 5.0 per cent, and in Coventry 7.4 per cent, all less than the then national average, and mostly less than half the June rates for 1984. Only the North-West, including Vauxhall's Ellesmere Port, and Ford's Halewood plants had, and still have, unemployment rates well above the national average.

Of the continental car-producing countries, only West Germany has a strong apprenticeship system giving rise to transferable skills. In both France and Italy, firms rely more upon in-house training and upgrading to fill skilled positions, and consequently skilled workers there find that their skills often do not match vacancies in other firms. Moreover, if these other firms also use upgrading, then displaced skilled workers face a period of lower pay in a less skilled position if made redundant, and considerable difficulty in getting another skilled job. The immigrant workers to be made redundant at Peugeot's Poissy plant in 1983–84 faced limited transferability of their skills on local labour markets, compounded by fear of discrimination in job hunting.

In addition, in all three countries, the rewards for long-service manual workers are at least double those in Britain. The New Earnings Survey showed only an 8.7 per cent differential in weekly earnings between short- and long-service workers in the industry, slightly above the position for manufacturing as a whole. In the car industry in France, the equivalent earnings differential was 35 per cent, in Italy 18 per cent, and in West Germany 15 per cent.[3]

A second factor accounting for the lesser difficulty of obtaining redundancies in Britain may be that because of the history of adjustment to variations in the labour demand of individual firms through local labour markets, British workers have not developed the expectation of long-term employment security. Whereas worker representation in France, West Germany, and Sweden is organized around the industry and the enterprise, British unions to a greater extent retain the occupational group, and thus the occupational labour market, as a basis for organization.

Because the car companies have often sought to cut employment without corresponding reductions in output levels, improving working and manning practices, and adapting to new technology were crucial. This caused some notable changes in the occupational structure of the labour force, and it is to these that we now turn.

CHANGES IN OCCUPATIONAL STRUCTURE

Previous chapters have indicated three main sources of change in the occupational mix in the car industry: new technology, increased efficiency, and the decline in the amount of engineering and design work undertaken in Britain. GM now undertakes much of this work for passenger cars outside Britain, as does Talbot. BL has subcontracted some of its design and engineering work abroad, and in some of the recent collaborative ventures with Japan, this work has been provided by the Japanese. Ford too divides its European design work between Britain and West Germany. Technical change is likely to have caused the skill mix to shift from production to maintenance work, and from mechanical to more electrical, electronic, and hydraulic skills. Increased efficiency should have reduced employment in those areas identified by the companies as overmanned, notably in assembly work. The decline in engineering and design work would mostly affect engineers and certain skills such as the tool-room and draughtsmen, but it could also reduce the growth of occupations which would have benefited from technical change in this area.

Throughout much of the 1970s, the broad occupational structure in the industry changed little, until about 1978–79, when the big employment reductions began. In absolute terms, employment declined in all occupations, but it declined faster for semi-skilled and unskilled workers, and for clerical and secretarial staff. The employment share of managerial and technical occupations rose, while that of craftsmen remained stable. The results of three different surveys need to be brought together to follow these changes.

The most detailed picture of the occupational mix in the industry comes from the 1971 and 1981 population censuses (*Table 6*). A less detailed picture of year-to-year changes up

OHP

Table 6 *Occupations*[a] *in the car industry*[b] *in 1971 and 1981*

occupation	per cent (M + F)		median age (men)	
	1971	1981	1971	1981
manual	80.2	76.0	—	—
non-manual	19.4	23.5	—	—
managers	2.5	3.7	45.2	43.4
personnel management, work study	0.6	0.5	—	—
sales and marketing	0.4	1.4	41.8	49.9
mechanical engineers	0.8	1.4	38.2	37.0
engineers not elsewhere classified and technologists	0.5	2.1	35.2	38.9
electrical and electronic engineers	0.1	0.1	—	—
draughtsmen	1.3	0.9	34.3	32.4
laboratory assistants and technicians	1.5	0.7	—	—
clerks	6.7	5.4	45.2	45.4
typists, office machine operators	2.8	2.4	—	—
foremen	2.5	} 3.4	46.8	45.9
apprentices	0.8		—	—
electricians	1.3	1.9	36.4	36.5
toolmakers	2.3	2.4	38.1	35.7
sheet metal workers	2.0	1.8	40.4	38.5
plumbers and pipe fitters	0.3	0.4	—	—
welders	3.2	3.4	37.5	37.5
motor mechanics	1.0	1.8	34.1	34.5
fitters (maintenance and not elsewhere classified)	7.4	5.9	40.2	38.1
machine tool setters, operators, turners	14.9	12.8	41.2	42.4
press, stamp operators, etc.	2.0	0.4	39.7	41.6
inspectors	4.9	} 5.9	48.5	} 46.3
packers, bottlers	0.8		46.2	
repetitive assemblers, etc.	10.5	7.3	37.6	38.3
labourers	5.2	3.1	49.1	46.5
security	0.6	0.7	—	—
catering	0.6	0.4	—	—
% in matched occupations	77.5	70.2		

Source: Census of Population 1971 and 1981; 1971 SIC (1968: 381); 1981 SIC (1980: 35) motor vehicles and parts.

Notes:

a The occupations shown are those which could be matched between 1971 and 1981.

b Numbers employed in 1979 in SIC (1968: 381) were 482,500, and in SIC (1980: 35) 491,200. SIC (1968: 381) includes manufacture of gears and transmission equipment (SIC 1980: 326) (Source: Census of Production 1979).

to 1979 is provided by the Department of Employment's (DE) survey of occupations in engineering, and for 1979 to 1984 by the Engineering Industry Training Board's (EITB) survey (*Table 7*). These are referred to respectively as the DE and the EITB

Table 7 *Employment by occupation in the motor vehicles and parts industry, 1978–84*

occupation	1978	1981	1984
	%	%	%
managerial staff	2.7	3.9	4.7
scientists and technologists	0.6	1.0	1.1
technicians and draughtsmen	4.3	5.2	5.8
administration and professional staff	4.3	5.2	6.2
clerks, office machine operators, secretaries, and typists	7.1	7.0	6.2
supervisors and foremen	4.8	5.0	4.8
craftsmen	14.1	15.7	15.8
operators	36.0	37.2	55.5
others	26.1	19.9	
numbers	448,466	339,632	261,415

Source: EITB, Sector Profile, Motor Vehicles and Parts Manufacturing, April, 1984.

surveys. The comparisons relate to motor vehicle manufacture (including parts) (SIC 1968: 381; 1980: 35). The main difference between the two industry classifications is the inclusion in 1971 of the manufacture of gears and transmission equipment (SIC 1980: 326).[1]

The employment share of male craftsmen stood at 25.7 per cent in May, 1973, and at 26.3 per cent in May, 1979, while 'other production' (including most assembly operations) workers went from 38.9 per cent to 37.8 per cent, and foremen went from 3.9 per cent to 4.5 per cent, and there was little year-to-year variation. In addition, the percentage of women showed little variation outside 12–13 per cent of the labour force. The DE survey therefore shows there was little major change in the broad occupational structure of the industry throughout the 1970s, the only clear trend being the gradual increase in the percentage of foremen. This is corroborated by a separate DE survey of manual workers' earnings in engineering occupations.[4] The two main trends to note in this survey through the 1970s were the steady growth in the share of maintenance fitters and electricians to 2.1 per cent and 1.6 per cent respectively of manual men in June, 1980, the pace of change having increased between 1979 and 1980, and the steady decline of the tool-room between 1975 and 1979 from 4 per cent to 3 per cent of manual men.

The population censuses of 1971 and 1981 give a more detailed picture despite a change of occupational classification. Because there was little overall change between 1973 and 1979, many of the changes recorded between the two censuses probably occurred between 1979 and 1981. Again the overall picture is not one of dramatic change in the occupations employed by the industry. Since 1981, a number of important technical changes have occurred, including the introduction of the highly automated Sierra line and the opening of the Brigend engine plant at Ford, and the changes at BL's Cowley plant, plus increased use of computer-aided engineering. Nevertheless, the census would have picked up the changes at Longbridge, and the retooling of Halewood for the new Escort. The EITB data for 1981 to 1984 show that although employment of all groups declined in absolute terms, the employment share of managers, technicians, and administrative and professional (mostly engineers and scientists) staff continued to increase. The share of craftsmen and of scientists and technologists remained stable, while that of semi-skilled and unskilled workers, and of clerical and secretarial staff continued to decline.

The impact of technical change, and the increased awareness of the need to keep abreast of new developments in both the product and the process can be seen in a number of changes. These may be reflected in the growth in the proportion of management and of engineers although it has been partly offset by the decline in the amount of design and product engineering work done in Britain over the last few years. In contrast to the census data, the EITB survey shows a sharp increase in the employment share of technicians between 1978 and 1984, up from 4.5 per cent to 5.8 per cent (*Table* 7). As the census shows that draughtsmen lost employment share, these figures understate the rise of technicians.

There has been some increase in employment share in certain maintenance and other non-production skills, notably electricians, whose share was up by half. The census shows a slight increase in the share of welders, mechanics, and tool-room workers. There is, however, a discrepancy between the DE engineering earnings survey and the census on the decline or otherwise in employment share for tool-room workers. The first source excludes small establishments (with less than twenty-five employees), while the census does not. It is possible that some tool-room workers left the large car plants for smaller component ones. Technical change may have affected the tool-room sooner in the large firms on account of their greater resources for investment.

The moves towards 'self-inspection' by production workers and the greater ease of automated inspection and quality control, which have taken place at all the major car producers are not apparent in the census data. There are three main reasons for this: some self-inspection enables redeployment of specialist inspectors to other inspection tasks; the census data also cover the car components sector in which changes have been slower to come about; and finally, the 1981 census figure includes both inspectors and a significant proportion of packers and bottlers.

The introduction of CAD has reduced jobs for draughtsmen as it saves the repeated redrawing of plans for particular parts of the car each time a modification of design is made. Some groups of skilled workers have also been adversely affected, notably production skills such as sheet metal workers, machine tool setter operators, and fitters. The 1981 census understates the decline in the share of non-maintenance fitters because that of maintenance fitters (about one-fifth of all fitters in the 1971 census) actually increased during the 1970s according to the DE earnings survey. Press and stamp operators have been affected by the introduction of automated stamps and presses, less dramatic but as far-reaching as multi- and robot-welders.

But the biggest changes in occupational mix arose from the drive for increased efficiency. Major reductions have occurred in employment share for assembly workers, labourers, and clerical and secretarial staff. The assemblers have been affected partly by automation, but more substantially by changes in working practices on the line, and in improvements in car design to make assembly work easier.

The burden of productivity improvements has fallen upon direct labour, and less upon maintenance and white-collar staff. Thus the main effort of getting manning levels more competitive has disproportionately affected blue-collar production jobs, and despite reductions in absolute terms, the employment share of non-manual workers has increased from just under a fifth to just under a quarter of the industry's labour force.

The decline in the median age of labourers reflects the elimination of older unskilled workers through early retirement and of the jobs they did. Many would have occupied less productive jobs reserved for older employees no longer able or wishing to keep up with line speeds.

To conclude, the period up to about 1979 saw little major change in the occupational mix in the industry, and it is only since then that most changes have occurred. While providing a convenient benchmark for comparison with 1971, the 1981 census may understate some of the changes in progress, but the broad changes, and their gradual nature are confirmed up to 1984 by the EITB survey. While it has captured the effects of the greater part of the 'shake out', it may have come too early for some of the effects of technical change. Nevertheless, the absence of any dramatic change in the occupational mix by 1981 must serve as a warning against exaggerated accounts of the impact of technical change. The EITB data show no change in the employment share of craftsmen in the industry between 1981 and 1984, but give no details of changes within individual occupations. The small changes in the average age of men in these occupations between 1971 and 1981 further reinforces this conclusion. While technical change should not be underestimated, it would seem that the greater part of the change in occupational mix up to 1981 arose from improvements in efficiency, and to a lesser extent from the decline in the amount of engineering work done in the UK.

CHANGES IN RELATIVE EARNINGS

The industry's ability to recruit from local labour markets between the 1950s and the middle 1970s arose in part from its high levels of pay as compared with other types of manual work. In April, 1972, manual men's weekly earnings in the industry (SIC: 381) stood 18 per cent above the average for manual men in manufacturing industries (New Earnings Survey). By 1975 their differential had fallen by more than two-thirds, and by 1981 average weekly earnings had fallen to 1 or 2 per cent below the manufacturing average, but recovered partially to 5 per cent above the average in 1984. Although employment levels in the industry recovered somewhat after the first oil shock, earnings relative to the rest of manufacturing continued to decline. A similar decline down the industrial earnings league happened to the Italian, and to a lesser extent the French, car workers. In contrast, in West Germany, the pay position of the early 1970s was maintained, as it was in the USA.

If, as has been suggested, the occupational mix, and the nature of the occupations in the industry has not changed a great deal, then the drop in relative pay might be expected to lead to future problems of labour retention, unless other policies are substituted for high pay, such as linking pay to length of service, or creating opportunities for job progression – policies often associated with the development of companies' internal labour markets. These problems should be greater for the plants in labour markets with lower unemployment rates, such as Oxford, Dagenham, and Luton, than in others such as Longbridge, and in particular Halewood and Ellesmere Port.

PRESSURES TOWARDS THE DEVELOPMENT OF INTERNAL LABOUR MARKETS

There have been a number of general economic pressures which might, other things being equal, be thought likely to push companies towards greater development of their internal labour markets. In some cases, these might also push towards greater emphasis upon employee participation, or at least involvement. It might be expected that the introduction of microelectronic technology has generated a demand for skills which are not readily provided by local labour markets so that companies have had to develop their own training programmes, or to rely upon training by the suppliers of new equipment. In either case, the employer generally has to pay for training, and so is likely to seek ways of retaining such workers. Second, new technology often makes old skill demarcations obsolete, especially in maintenance work, and reduces the demand for transferable skills formerly provided by apprenticeships in the car firms. Third, the strong emphasis upon flexibility of deployment of workers between jobs within the company is again going to push employers towards developing management systems to deal with such internal redeployment, and to seek to design job descriptions and job classifications appropriately. Fourth, the development of enlarged jobs for assembly workers involving, for example, a degree of routine maintenance and inspection work is also likely to increase individual workers' investment in company-related skills, again increasing the premium on internally generated skills. Fifth, the general increased emphasis upon training, especially for semi-skilled workers, as a means of improving quality and increasing adaptability also places a premium for the employer on a stable work-force. Indeed, in Sweden, as well as in Britain, the reduced labour turnover compared with the early and mid-1970s made training much more attractive to employers.

Finally, the ability to redeploy labour within internal labour markets depends upon the existence of job and grading structures, and work rules which facilitate this. Before the late 1970s, the US car industry offered an example of rigid internal labour markets as seniority rules developed in collective agreements to regulate lay-offs and upgrading had created rigid job ladders between which redeployment of labour was difficult. These rules intensified a system of highly specialized job classifications used by management. The seniority rules which characterize this type of internal labour market were designed to control job insecurity, and although they did nothing to reduce it overall, they introduced a degree of predictability. Thus one important idea is that the labour force is much more likely to accept increased job flexibility if the companies offer in exchange some form of employment security.

Such a trade-off cannot be pursued in isolation from other personnel policies. It can be reinforced by some form of increased worker participation or employee involvement. Such provisions would be intended to complement orthodox collective bargaining, giving employees a chance to influence the relevant decisions, and to engender a degree of mutual trust required to ensure continued flexibility. The link between these two is, however, contingent and not necessary. Before pursuing this question in the British context, it is worth looking at some of the developments in other long-standing car producing countries.

Summarizing the experience of several European countries, the USA, and Japan, Katz and Streeck (1984) outlined two broad strategies between which companies and unions in the industry might choose in order to deal with restructuring. The first was a co-operative strategy based upon the idea that increased flexibility of working practices and acceptance of new technology required some form of increased job security for workers remaining with the firm, combined with greater consultation and worker participation. This was partly inspired by increased awareness of Japanese practices, and partly by building on existing experience in the countries concerned. The second strategy, which they characterized as 'neo-liberal', relied more upon a reassertion of managerial control over day-to-day work questions, based to some extent upon a reassertion of market pressures. There is a heavy emphasis upon removing rigidities within labour markets, the prime source of these being identified with protection of existing working practices and established wage structures. While it would be a mistake to see these as polar opposites, they nevertheless represent strong differences of emphasis.

Those pressures pushing towards further development of internal labour markets also seem to have favoured the development of more participative institutional structures in certain countries. Thus in Germany, Sweden, and the USA, the car employers seem to have reacted to these pressures by reinforcing their internal labour markets, and developing forms of employee consultation. Hoff (1983) describes the system of consultation and information provision developed within Audi after 1978 to discuss the employment implications of the company's investment plans. This would improve the works council's ability to negotiate for greater redeployment and retraining within the company in the event of major readjustments, and generally provide a more effective vehicle through which work-force pressures can be exerted over employment questions; in particular it would be likely to improve the position of current employees *vis-à-vis* other workers in applying for vacancies within the company. Similarly, Brumlop and Jurgens (1983) placed considerable stress upon the development of consultation over new equipment generally within VW, and the works council's acceptance of the need for flexibility and retraining.

In Sweden, Peterson (1983) argued that Volvo would continue with and extend its 'internal labour market' strategy, partly because of the expectation that its labour force was unlikely to grow in the coming years, but also because of recognition of the need for flexibility in jobs in response to both new technology, and to productivity pressures. He argued that the company's emphasis upon employment security for its current employees was an essential means for getting flexibility for the introduction of new technology. Consequently there was a heavy emphasis upon training and retraining within the company, and the development of vertical mobility among non-manual workers. This was managed through participation, as in the 1983 agreement on efficiency and participation.

Some of the most remarkable changes have occurred in the USA, and according to Katz (1983, 1984) these represented a major break with past management practices. There it was more a case of the employers seeking to reorganize their internal labour markets than to increase their scope. Important examples arising from the 1982 contract with the UAW were the guarantees of an income stream for a period for certain workers laid off and thus recognized for the first time as having been permanently laid off; the pilot employment guarantees offered to workers in the industry, and the industry's national employee development and training programme. Katz argued that the first increased the cost of redundancies to the employer and so placed a premium upon forward manpower planning, while the second directly contributed to the companies' internal labour markets. These guarantees were offered in exchange for concessions on labour costs, the annual improvement factor and cost of living adjustments, and for concessions of working practices, notably the rigidities in labour allocation within the firm imposed by the seniority districts for upgrading and lay-offs. As the seniority rules were intended to protect workers against arbitrary lay-offs, to win acceptance for some relaxation in their application would require some alternative protection. This could explain in part the experiments with employment guarantees, but it could also explain the development in many plants of employee involvement, and of quality circles, thus establishing a link between reinforcing internal labour markets and aspects of the 'co-operative strategy'.

These moves were taken further in the agreements reached between the UAW and GM and Ford in November, 1984. In exchange for greater job flexibility the agreements offered extended employment security provisions, mainly in the form of a long-term training and redeployment programme. At GM, the scheme covered all employees with more than one year's service. The company would be free to cut up to 100,000 jobs, and under-scheme employees would maintain their income while retraining for new jobs inside or outside the company. The Ford agreement was similar, but the guarantees less far-reaching.

The evidence from West Germany, Sweden, and the USA that internal labour markets have been extended and reinforced needs to be taken with some care. The implicit or explicit employment guarantees fall a long way short of the Japanese 'lifetime employment system', but they nevertheless indicate the direction in which some firms in these countries have been moving.

INTERNAL LABOUR MARKETS IN BRITAIN

Employers in the British car industry have not really moved in the same direction as some of their West German, Swedish, and North American counterparts of reinforcing their internal labour markets by offering increased job security in exchange for greater job flexibility. Moreover, the recent position taken by the Engineering Employers' Federation (EEF) in their 1983 annual negotiations with the engineering unions shows that other engineering employers are following similar lines to the British car producers. In response to the unions' demand for a shorter working week, the employers set out demands for flexible working time patterns; no industrial action to be taken without a ballot; the removal of obstacles to efficiency; and revised implementation arrangements.

A number of tests indicate that British companies have not been reinforcing their internal labour markets, but maintaining their links with local skilled labour markets, unlike other countries. First, in Britain, the content of skills developed for working with the newly introduced robotic equipment are thought by BL managers to be about 75 per cent transferable, especially as the technology diffuses to other firms in the same local labour markets. This is particularly likely for the car firms with plants in the Midlands engineering belt, notably BL, but less likely for those with plants in areas in which the engineering industry is less well represented, such as the Liverpool area where Ford and Vauxhall have major car plants. One of the chief reasons for the high degree of transferability is that existing skills have been extended to cater for new technology so that many craft skills, and the craft/semi-skilled divide, far from being displaced are in fact being enhanced. The higher degree of transferability may be maintained in Britain unlike elsewhere because new skills have often been grafted on to the existing organization of skilled work.

A second indication that they have not reinforced their

internal labour markets to the extent of other countries lies in the limited changes in the organization of skilled work in British industry, as already shown by the small degree of change in the industry's occupational mix. This pattern of organization relies heavily upon an apprenticeship system, but unlike the apprenticeship system in West Germany, it regulates not just the acquisition of technical competence, but also access to craft work. Whereas the key to the West German apprenticeships and skilled work lies in access to technical competence, the pattern of regulation in Britain relies more on access to 'job territories', that is sets of tasks and the use of certain tools which are the exclusive right of certain groups of workers. The skills established in this way are mostly transferable between firms, so that they are geared towards their local labour markets. A central aspect of adaptation of skills to new technology lies in the way in which such skill demarcations are adjusted. In both Ford and Vauxhall there has been relatively little change in craft demarcations, and thus little reason to believe that such skills have lost much of their transferability.

In BL, where craft work has perhaps changed the most, the introduction of flexibility of deployment in the maintenance area by the principle of 'two-trades response' to maintenance problems on its most automated lines has involved almost exclusively changes in job boundaries between existing groups of craftsmen, but no change between craft and semi-skilled. The principle of two-trades response involves the use of a craftsman with electrical/electronics skills plus one with mechanical skills. Nevertheless, the individual craftsmen retain their craft affiliation, and the electrical, mechanical, and pipe fitting trades retain their separate identity in training. In all three firms, development of electronics skills, which are not entirely new in any case, has been largely on the principle that the existing base of skills should be adapted, where possible, by the addition of new training modules (so that additional electronics skills would go to electricians or the appropriate mechanical crafts) rather than by the development of people with specialist skills related to a single piece of equipment. The latter would have skills which would quickly become obsolete, and would not usually have the necessary knowledge base from which to develop new skills.

Third, among semi-skilled workers, one of the areas of job enlargement which might be thought to lead employers to place a higher value on labour force stability has been that of 'self-inspection' and 'self-maintenance', both ideas acquiring a certain popularity because of Japanese methods. Mostly self-inspection has enabled firms to reduce the number of specialist inspectors, and in the process eliminate one of the traditional forms of upward job mobility for older semi-skilled workers. In one sense, this might be thought to reduce the scope for internal labour markets. However, self-inspection has been part of the general philosophy of 'get it right first time', that is of reducing the frequency with which work is sent back for rectification, a highly labour intensive and costly process. The other element has been that of 'self-maintenance', but it should be clear from the discussion of maintenance craft demarcations that this in fact involves little more than petty unskilled maintenance, mostly oiling and cleaning up. Thus, the impact of these on the development of internal labour markets has been fairly limited.

Fourth, although there has been an increased training input into semi-skilled work, which might be thought to increase the premium on labour force stability it has not been such as to enhance the firms' internal labour markets. This training has been an important element of the improved quality control involving, for example, a much more systematic approach towards showing semi-skilled workers how to do their job, and what it should look like when completed. While the amount of training now received by any individual semi-skilled worker may not be very great, the overall investment by the company has to be multiplied by the number of workers receiving it. Clearly, high rates of labour turnover could greatly increase training costs. However, on the whole, these do not seem to have led to the development of the highly structured sequences of jobs and training, through which workers might progress, that are typical of some kinds of internal labour market. Moreover, one result of high levels of unemployment has been to reduce labour turnover (noted also in Sweden [Peterson 1983]), and this has facilitated the employers' investment in training without creating the need for elaborate personnel policies to tie workers to the firm.

Finally, one must consider the flexibility of redeployment within companies, which is a characteristic of some internal labour markets. But this has been heavily related to the companies' redundancy programmes, so it is hard to tell whether it represents a permanent shift in patterns of deployment. Firms have nevertheless had to develop new personnel practices in order to manage such redeployment, and to establish negotiating structures to deal with it. Examples would be BL's computerized manpower resourcing information system at Longbridge, which provides the information necessary for management to deploy labour more easily, and Vauxhall's changes in their job and pay grade structures, using fewer and broader pay bands, in order to facilitate transfers of labour within the plant. These may well prepare the way for a more permanent change.

Thus, while there has been some move towards a reinforcement of internal labour markets in Britain, it would appear to have been limited. British employers, in the car industry at least, do not appear to have followed the pattern of German, Swedish, or North American employers. Yet despite pursuing a different path, several companies in Britain claim to have achieved major productivity improvements, either eliminating or greatly reducing the productivity gap which separated them from their West European counterparts in the 1970s. BL and Vauxhall claim to have made major, and Ford more limited, advances in this direction.

REASONS FOR THE LOCAL LABOUR MARKET ORIENTATION OF BRITISH EMPLOYERS AND UNIONS

What have been the reasons for the different type of strategies followed by employers in Britain, compared with the other countries? The first reason would seem to be that although internal labour markets functioning in the light of the Japanese experience appear to provide a great deal of flexibility in allocation of labour between jobs, one should not overlook the different kind of labour force flexibility that can be provided by local labour market structures, as was illustrated earlier in the material on employment fluctuations in the post-war period. Moreover, many workers have invested in skills adapted to this kind of structure, so that the cost to companies of negotiating a major change, even if they wanted to, would be considerable. Another factor has been the focus of plant-based negotiating machinery on individual jobs and work groups (partly because of the 'job-territory' system), and the difficulty experienced by British unions in developing strong centralized plant and company level organizations, their strength being focused at a lower level. In the car industry, but also in steel, previous experiences in high level worker participation did not lead to changes in workers' attitudes or to increased flexibility.

The flexibility of internal labour markets with relatively unrestricted managerial prerogative is perhaps best illustrated by the Japanese case where the main constraint on job demarcation and the adaptation of job structures to new technology seems to be technical competence, and safety. This strategy tends to make labour costs, for the core labour force at least, into an overhead. However, local labour markets can also provide flexibility, but of a different kind, through the greater ease of expanding a company's skilled labour force, as lead times in recruitment decisions are shorter than if a skilled person has to be trained, and through the greater readiness of workers to accept lay-offs, as their skills are more easily transferable. It could be argued that some of the rigidity of skill demarcations arises from the desire of skilled workers to retain the transferability of their skills rather than adapt to a specialism only used by their current employer. This may make adaptation to technical change slower because of the greater amount of negotiation required for changes in job descriptions, but the other associated forms of flexibility through the possibility of inter-firm mobility should not be overlooked. Britain and West Germany are probably alone of the major car producing countries to have such well-developed local labour markets for skilled labour, and this may prove to be an important factor in determining which type of strategy is chosen.

Moreover, in the British car industry, the craft unions (including craft sections of larger unions) are acutely aware of the importance of maintaining the marketability or transfer-ability of their skills. Some evidence of this can be found in their fears that BL will move away from the established system of apprenticeships governed by the EITB towards a system of 'certification'. They feared two aspects of this. First, a move away from the industry-wide standards established by the EITB towards certified standards determined by individual employers would make the resulting skills less marketable. The second was that this would involve a move away from the present modular system under which apprentices taking training modules in two specialisms (for example as a mechanical and as a machine tool fitter), towards one in which the second module would not be guaranteed and could be left to later. The craft unions again feared that this would lead to a dilution of craft skills and again to a loss of their marketability. From the employers' point of view the main advantages would seem to be that skills could be more closely adapted to their own particular needs, and there would be less concentration of training into the initial period of a person's working life than under the existing apprenticeship system, which many employers believe increases its cost and reduces its flexibility at a time of major technical change. Thus it appears that the craft unions see this issue as one of defence of their craft labour market and are keenly aware of need to maintain the transferability of their skills. Further evidence of such concern can be seen in the EETPU's (the electricians' union) decision to provide electronics training to its members to ensure that a broad enough range of skills is acquired, and in recent moves by the AUEW following the electricians' example.

Over and above the cost of additional training required, the extent to which employers seek greater flexibility in skill demarcations in Britain is limited by the likely cost of negotiating them. Thus there has generally been a preference for a lower cost strategy of negotiating changes in some of the more peripheral tasks in job territories. This is particularly true of those tasks which have become traditionally part of one craft's job territory but which do not require the exercise of any special competence or judgement. In this way, firms can reduce the number of craftsmen required to be present in any particular maintenance job.

The key position of craft maintenance skills in the skill hierarchy restricts any attempt to base internal labour markets upon any extensive system of job progression. Instead, for most operatives, job movements are confined to moves within the same job grade, as upgrading opportunities are mostly constrained by the small number of semi-skilled grades. For their manual workers, Ford and BL have a five-grade structure of which the top grade is confined to craftsmen, and although Vauxhall's system is more complex, its broad principles are the same. The highest upgrading for semi-skilled workers is usually to inspector, but with the increasing move towards direct inspection by semi-skilled operatives (self-inspection), plus the amount of self-inspection built into some new equipment, even these opportunities are decreasing.

There have been some changes affecting demarcations around maintenance work, but there appears to have been very little movement on the divide between semi-skilled and craft jobs beyond very limited amounts of routine maintenance. Between craft skills, like many other employers, the car producers have been keen to relax demarcations rather than abolish them, pressing for greater flexibility around the edge of job territories, and for a greater degree of overlap between them so that less individual trades are required to be present for any particular piece of maintenance work. The most widely publicized and most dramatic changes in demarcations between craft skills have perhaps occurred at BL with the development of two-trades response to deal with maintenance problems, but there may well be limits on the degree of flexibility in demarcations that would be desirable on economic grounds. It is clearly important that incompetent and unsafe maintenance work should be avoided, both because of workers' safety, and because of the cost of the equipment involved. At the same time, training every worker in all aspects of maintenance would be extremely costly. This problem, of course, is not unique to Britain.

These last points justify continued specialization among maintenance-skilled workers, but they do not necessarily point to use of local labour markets instead of developing specialist 'repair men' with the skills necessary for the maintenance of particular pieces of equipment (similar, for example, to xerox machine engineers who may combine both limited fitting and electrical skills, but related to a specific piece of equipment). First, technology is changing fairly quickly so that the companies' and the individual workers' investment in such skills would soon become obsolete. Second, in the longer run such skills may be less adaptable than general electrical or other skills to which specialist modules can be added while retaining the basic general skill. Although companies can and do build on existing skills, it is easier to do this on the basis of solid training in general principles than on simple familiarity with operating certain pieces of equipment. Third, and perhaps most important, retaining the established system of apprenticeships, and the established local labour markets for such skills, leaves employers and workers with the flexibility associated with the local labour market. Moreover, on the crucial question as to who should receive additional electronics training, the companies appear to have followed the principle that this should go to those who are already fully qualified craftsmen. This has probably been the line of least resistance both in terms of collective bargaining, and of the costs of investment in training. In addition, since the manpower reductions, the companies have also had numbers of craftsmen needing redeployment.

Use of local labour markets for recruitment at all levels of skill, as in the British car industry, does not mean that companies simply pursue a policy of 'hire and fire' coupled with short job tenure. Despite heavy use of early retirement as an alternative to redundancies, in all three major car companies the median length of service of male manual workers currently with the companies is between 10 and 12 years. This is equivalent to a typical completed length service, on retirement or on leaving the company, of the order of 15–20 years. Moreover, length of service of manual workers in the industry was above the average for manufacturing even in the mid-1970s before the job losses.[5]

These high length of service figures for a major part of the labour force cannot be explained simply by the investment in training of individuals in view of the small amount of initial training that is required for semi-skilled assembly work: up to about two weeks. However, despite the highly individualized nature of many tasks in car assembly, there is a sense in which investment is made in the skills of the work-force as a whole, and in its ability to work as a unit. In addition, the more individual workers have experience of several tasks, the more easily they can be moved between operations making for a more flexible work-force. Although each individual worker can be replaced by someone recruited directly from the local labour market, the process depends upon there being sufficient stability in the work-force as a whole for the communication of the necessary technical and social skills. High rates of labour turnover could impede this, and it is possible that some of the quality problems encountered in the mid-1970s were connected with the high turnover rates experienced then.

In addition, internal job mobility within the British car firms is not associated with much increase in earnings. This is in part a consequence of the system of pay grades with between five and seven grades for hourly paid workers depending on the company. As craftsmen occupy the top grade, this effectively leaves little room for earnings progression through upgrading for semi-skilled workers.

Thus the pattern of labour market organization in Britain appears to militate against further consolidation of internal labour markets on the lines suggested in a number of other countries. This is compounded by the advantage employers can derive from local labour market flexibility (through horizontal rather than vertical labour mobility), and because employers have been able to obtain a certain amount of job flexibility without seeking to dismantle the craft system. In addition, this system is also important in union organization.

As mentioned earlier, the pattern of bargaining is related to the organization of skilled work, and its orientation to local labour markets and their occupational categories. It has been argued (Marsden 1980) that basing the craft system upon job territories as distinct from the exercise of a particular technical competence both provides a model for the organization of other occupational groups within the firm, and provides an incentive for them to do so, as groups failing to do so may be squeezed out by other groups. Reliance upon job territories does not preclude a high level of technical competence, but narrowly specifying the set of tasks over which this competence may be exercised means that smaller changes in work organiza-tion required by technical or other changes trigger off negotiations than would be the case where the exercise of technical competence is the defining feature of a job. To be sure, even skilled occupations defined by technical competence may become obsolete, and may require adaptation, which in West Germany is usually handled by negotiation and can be the occasion of conflict, but the threshold of negotiation is higher, and it can be conducted in more abstract terms through the works council (see Maurice, Sellier, and Silvestre 1978). In Britain, the highly detailed way in which such changes are framed because one is dealing with execution of individual tasks means that it is difficult to deal with such questions in terms of general principles, and that the level of negotiation most appropriate to dealing with such changes is very close to the job. This is one reason for the vitality of shop steward bargaining. It would also be very difficult to deal with such questions in the more abstract way in which they might be framed within a German works council. Thus the system of craft and occupational organization in much of British industry favours the highly decentralized pattern of representation through shop stewards as against more centralized company institutions.

There is an additional link between the patterns of skill and union organization, namely that the craft system, being oriented towards regulation of local labour markets rather than responding to a logic of company-based organization, favours a form of occupational unionism. In one sense there is a single-union structure for occupations, but a multi-union structure in individual industries and firms. Industrial unionism in West Germany leads to multi-unionism within occupations, as, for example, electricians in the chemical, construction, mining, and engineering industries would be in different unions.

CONCLUSIONS

Employment in the British car industry was greatly reduced between 1979 and 1982, after which the job losses slowed but have not entirely ceased. The main reasons, apart from the drop in output, were the need to get productivity levels nearer to those of continental European, and especially West German, plants. For BL this has been necessary in order to survive as a commercial enterprise, and although in theory Ford and GM could supply their British markets from their European and other overseas plants, there are many practical problems preventing this. The job losses have arisen in part from plant closures, but the greater part, for BL, Ford, and Vauxhall have come from demanning of plants that were to remain in operation. The necessary counterpart to such demanning has been reorganization of management and of jobs. Although fear of unemployment may reduce unions' bargaining power, the companies' need to reorganize and restructure compensates this for loss of power to some extent as the work-force has considerable blocking power. This has been reflected in the negotiations over redundancies, which have, apart from closures, been almost all on a voluntary basis.

The main changes in occupational mix in the industry in recent years have arisen out of technical change, but especially out of the moves to increase efficiency. The decline in the employment share of semi-skilled operatives and labourers visible in comparing the 1971 and 1981 census occurred mostly between 1979 and 1981, a time when only a few of the new production facilities had been introduced. Technical change may become a more influential factor now the major employment reductions in the four firms' main plants have been obtained. The other notable change in occupational structure has been the increase in the employment share of managers and of technical white-collar occupations. Craftsmen have about maintained their employment share. The main influence at work would seem to be the increase in the technical expertise required for modern car production.

The impact upon skills so far has been to enhance the position of craftsmen as a whole in the manual labour force, although tool-makers have lost share, and electricians expanded theirs. Changing skill boundaries, where it has occurred, has been between different groups of craftsmen, but hardly at all between craftsmen and semi-skilled workers. New electronics skills have, on the whole, been added on to existing craft skills.

In Britain, as in other European countries and the USA there has been a heavy emphasis upon increasing flexibility of deployment of labour within the plant. In Britain this has involved, for example, the redesigning of grading structures in order to facilitate redeployment, the development of information systems for monitoring deployment, and great use of extra training. In this Britain is not unique, yet there is some reason to doubt that the industry in this country is moving towards the greater development of internal labour markets to the extent that some other countries are. There one motive has been that more secure employment can be offered in exchange for the acceptance of greater job flexibility. One of the reasons why the firms in Britain seem to be behaving rather differently is that the pattern of labour market organization is different, as Britain, more than any other of the countries except perhaps West Germany has a system of local occupational labour markets for skilled labour. Although these are currently under threat because of the recent collapse of apprentice intake, such labour markets offer employers the chance of direct recruitment of skilled labour when needed. They also offer workers the chance of moving between firms while retaining their level of skill.

However, access to such skilled jobs is restricted to those with apprenticeships, so that opportunities for upgrading semi-skilled workers to skilled positions are limited, more so than in the internal labour markets in the USA, French, or Italian, and even the West German car industries. Thus scope for developing internal labour markets based on opportunities for upgrading to skilled positions and above in Britain is very limited. Thus, in Britain, hope of upgrading cannot be offered to semi-skilled workers as an incentive to accepting greater flexibility of deployment, or can only be done so to a more limited extent than in the other countries. Moreover, in Britain, earnings progression with length of service is considerably less than in the continental European countries.

Many of the changes described in this chapter imply radical changes in working practices and in labour management methods. The next chapter examines the changes underlying the increased efficiency of labour utilization and increased flexibility of deployment of labour within the firms.

FIVE
WORKING
PRACTICES

INTRODUCTION

The increased efficiency of the British car industry since the late 1970s has been the result of three main factors: the closure of old plant and capacity; the introduction of new technology; and an extensive reorganization of management coupled with changes in working practices and industrial relations. While closures have undoubtedly contributed to the industry's improved performance, as was shown in Chapters 2 and 4, these were mostly concentrated in BL and Talbot, and even in these firms there were major improvements in efficiency in the plants which were retained. The introduction of new technology has also contributed to improved efficiency, but as shown in Chapter 3, it has brought radical changes only in certain areas of the production process. Moreover, Vauxhall doubled its productivity at its Luton plant between 1979 and 1983 without introducing any major technical changes. This leaves the third force behind improved efficiency, namely changes in organization and in working practices, which are the subject of this chapter.

Of their nature, changes in organization and working practices do not fall into any neat categories, and any divisions may seem a little artificial. Nevertheless, for the purposes of this chapter these will be divided into changes in management organization, changes in working practices, and changes in the industrial relations procedures regulating them.

Because these organizational changes are interrelated and have all been introduced in the same short space of time, it is not possible to demonstrate that any one major change was more important than the others, nor is it possible to apportion shares of the productivity increase to any measures taken individually. We therefore focus on those changes which managements thought were particularly significant. As will be clear in this chapter, there were some changes about whose contribution most of the managers interviewed agreed, and others about which their views were more diverse, especially in the procedural area. The importance of some of these changes was also accepted on the union side, as is illustrated by BL's joint productivity sub-committee discussed in this chapter.

This chapter deals first, and briefly, with the changes in management organization; then looks in more detail at changes in working practices as they affect the way people do their jobs; and then as they affect the procedural side of labour relations. In the management area, these changes include better co-ordination, better planning of stocks, a greater emphasis on design for ease of production, and more forward planning of assembly work. They also include attempts to change management structure and attitudes, for example, Vauxhall's moves to combat over-specialization within management, in Sir Michael Edwardes's changes in BL's management, and Ford's 'After Japan' campaign and the search for 'employee involvement'.

The changes in the way production jobs are done have not been confined to the car industry, as is illustrated by the Incomes Data Services (IDS) study (1981), although they have been slow to spread across manufacturing industry as a whole. Illustrations of the changes highlighted by managements include: greater flexibility of deployment between functions and between parts of the plant, facilitated by changes in the wage and grade structures; increased flexibility of job demarcations, such as BL's 'two-trades maintenance response', and Ford's reduction of demarcations among mechanical trades; greater flexibility in response to production problems, such as BL's use of team working, and Ford's emphasis upon preventive maintenance; the introduction of a degree of 'self-inspection' and 'self-maintenance' in assembly work; and an increased emphasis upon taking time out of jobs, upon training and upon getting things 'right first time'. Many of these changes are linked to changes in management organization, as, for example, the reduction of buffer stocks requires better management co-ordination as well as a reduction in stoppages.

Changes on the procedural side, and in industrial relations more generally, have been more controversial and more discussed, and among these a central question has been the reduction of shop steward power and of the amount of negotiation over job changes. The role of shop stewards in all four companies seems to have declined, but they remain central actors in work-place relations. This is partly because increased job flexibility has meant a reassertion of management prerogative in the day-to-day use of labour leaving stewards with less to do in all four companies.

The damaging effect of a strong shop steward organization on productivity is not self-evident. Indeed one of the arguments of the Donovan Commission on the reform of Britain's industrial relations was that shop steward bodies, if organized in the right way and provided with the necessary facilities, could facilitate good industrial relations. During the 1970s, managements in the industry had conceded, freely or under pressure, a number of measures which should have assisted work-place trade union organization, yet by the end of the decade they were sceptical of the benefits. One of the most dramatic and controversial changes of that period occurred at BL with the ending of 'mutuality' in 1980. Sir Michael Edwardes saw this as an unquestionable improvement in management efficiency. However, in Chapter 6, we suggest that although he may have been right about mutuality as it had developed at BL, the failure to replace it with adequate channels for workers' grievances may have contributed to the continuing problem of small strikes in that company.

Finally, there have been moves to develop alternative forms of contact between management and workers, as illustrated by Ford's pursuit of employee involvement and better information for employees, and Vauxhall's use of consultation. An important aim has been to facilitate the flow of ideas for further productivity improvements, and to engender a more co-operative relationship between workers and management. However, as mentioned earlier, such measures can also require significant changes in management style and organization.

Although the changes in productivity have been considerable, a constant theme in our interviews with management was that of 'doing better what we were doing before'. In other words, one should not look for radical changes in methods of work and organization. There is a high degree of continuity both in work and in labour relations. Taken individually, many of these changes may seem fairly insignificant, but taken together they go some way towards explaining the increased efficiency throughout the car industry.

Before looking at management changes it is helpful to get a more concrete idea of the way in which management and work-force responsibilities for change were seen in the late 1970s. Within the labour relations framework in the industry, the report of BL's joint productivity sub-committee illustrates both managements' and unions' views of where responsibility for certain changes lay without actually specifying what precise measures should be taken. Although efficiency at BL was at the time lower than in the other major car producers in Britain, both the CPRS (1975) and the House of Commons Expenditure Committee (1975) attest to the prevalence of similar problems in the other firms.

Any assumption that inefficiencies were simply a question of too many stoppages and excessive manning levels is misleading. The five main factors seen in the sub-committee's report as contributing to poor labour productivity in order of importance were:

1. an acceptance of a greater amount of allowed non-productive time by comparison with our competitors;
2. the practice of regularly exceeding that allowed non-productive time, due to industrial relations problems other than strikes, such as go-slows, arguments about mobility, or demarcation;
3. disputes;
4. a greater amount of relaxation allowance;

5. more generous time standards than competitors.

In putting forward the greater amount of non-productive time as a reason for the lower productivity than competitors, the BL sub-committee put the ball in management's court. They wrote: 'This is essentially management's responsibility to correct but management cannot succeed in making these corrections without help from all employees.'

The ways in which the committee sought to remove this comparative disadvantage give a picture of the way in which attempts to improve efficiency are multi-dimensional, often involve highly specific improvements, and are not necessarily dominated by industrial relations factors, at least in the narrow sense of that term. The committee pointed to the following examples:

Reason for allowed non-productive time	*Way to eliminate problem*
1. Quality of panels received necessitates some rectification before fitting into jig.	Insist on correct panels from supplier. (Management responsibility.)
2. Due to uncovered storage facilities, panels rust and require additional treatment.	Improve storage facilities. (Management responsibility – requires cash and space.)
3. Old plant and machinery retained due to decision to extend model life.	Need for clear model/volume policy and continuous replacement of plant and equipment. (Management responsibility – but often model life is extended because of cash shortage.)
4. Time required to repair breakdowns is based on current practices within maintenance departments.	Time could be reduced if there was less demarcation between trades and more preventive maintenance schedules were introduced. (Joint trade union and management responsibility.)

A similar procedure was adopted towards the second of the reasons for low relative productivity. Some of the examples given were:

Reason for exceeding the allowed non-productive time	*Way to eliminate problem*
1. Relaxation allowance is exceeded or taken when not earned.	Tighter control by management and supervision and acknowledgement by trade unions that relaxation allowance must be earned *first* before it can be taken.
2. Agreed late starts and early finishes regularly exceeded.	Tighter control by management and supervision.
3. Material shortages occur more frequently than allowed for, due to inadequate stocks in stores and between operations.	Better control of stocks. However, vulnerability to outside suppliers' problems, distance, weather, and the need to reduce the cash tied up in big stocks all affect this item.
4. Difficulty in redeploying labour which has no work on its own section because of a dispute elsewhere.	This cannot always be avoided but clear understandings on mobility of labour and willingness of employees to move to other jobs/areas will help considerably.
5. Output reduced due to working to rule or unofficial go-slow although men not actually on strike.	Use of procedure and an understanding of the damage these practices have on our ability to compete.

Although the report was not intended to be an exhaustive academic analysis of the causes of BL's productivity gap, one striking feature of the analysis is the proportion of items for which responsibility is attributed to management.

MANAGEMENT REORGANIZATION

In all firms managers are keen to point to what one production manager called 'the simple fact that we are doing things better and are better organized'. For example, work flow, stock control procedures, and production control have been considerably improved, overcoming past problems due, for example, to the unavailability of parts, and the use of trial and error in setting up the line as opposed to planning. The increasingly sophisticated use of computers for production modelling and control and for stock control has played an important part in tackling such problems, as has also investment in, for example, improved storage facilities, automated components delivery to tracks, and body stackers. But changes in labour management practices and policies have also played an important role.

To aid these the management structure has been considerably reformed, as at BL and Vauxhall, and training and organizational development programmes have been used. In 1981 Vauxhall adopted a matrix as opposed to a departmental structure in order to facilitate the better provision of certain services to different functions. This altered the relationship between the maintenance and production departments to facilitate more efficiency and integration. At Ford, the number of layers in the management hierarchy was reduced from eight to five, and greater responsibility for decision-making was devolved to lower levels. To achieve this, the plant manufacturing activities were divided into four areas (stamping, body construction, paint, trim and final assembly) each of which has an area manager responsible for all production, maintenance, quality control, and line feed activities. Each area manager works with a small team of specialists in each of those activities, and no longer has to refer up to central staff functions in the plant. Formerly, production managers had day-to-day responsibility for getting production out, but no direct access to these specialist services.

There is an important overlap between shop floor changes in management organization, which includes improvements in the timing and design of jobs, and management's increasing willingness to assert control over late starts and early finishes, and breaches of discipline. The former has both a procedural and substantive dimension. For example, at BL industrial engineering could not be fully effective as long as there was 'mutuality' – the principle that joint agreement should be reached before any changes in work organization were implemented. Prior to new standards being introduced it was felt that this procedure had to be removed. The substantive area involved redesigning jobs, with a view to reducing allowed non-productive time, reducing the time allowed for jobs, and rationalizing operations. So part of the increased labour productivity has come about because of this redesign, which in some cases has made the job easier. For example, at Vauxhall's Luton plant, raising parts of the assembly line to head height has enabled operators to work standing up instead of leaning over, and made it easier to move with a moving assembly line. There is, however, little evidence as yet of job redesign in the UK aimed at improvements in job satisfaction or enrichment. Developments at Saab in Sweden for example, where long cycle times have been introduced, can be contrasted with those at BL. Despite use of similar technology, the designers of the Metro decided to forego the introduction of similar arrangements (Willman and Winch 1985).

Another important area of management change, which has involved greater co-ordination between different levels of management, has been in the area of production engineering and control. Managements no longer allow disputes to be settled by concessions which impede efficient production. At Talbot, for example, where 40 per cent improvement in productivity in four years has been achieved, managers stressed the importance of continuous working, and the elimination of what they call 'petty' disputes, unofficial relief time, late starts and early finishes, as well as tighter manning assignments. Management had allowed such practices to develop in the late 1960s and early 1970s when they could sell all they could produce and the sole criterion was cars off the line. At Ford there was always a greater determination not to resolve short-term production difficulties 'by throwing labour at the line', as it is called in the industry.

There is also greater awareness among managers of the need to maintain quality, and not to sacrifice it to resolve temporary problems. This is in response to customer pressures, but it also has an important cost element. The emphasis on a high percentage 'right first time', now common to all UK manufacturers, is related to increased cost pressures: rectification work is costly, and is tantamount to inserting batch production into a mass production process. In an attempt to improve quality BL attacked the problem from two angles. The first, already discussed, was automation of welding. The second was the pursuit of higher quality and lower cost components through tighter control of supplies. In fact, this extended to an attempt to influence industrial relations within supplier companies – BL have continuously expressed the view that wage rises in supplier companies should not be passed on to component prices.

The requirement to co-ordinate process efficiency improvements of these types has led to a greater emphasis on discipline, and in particular on the authority of first-line supervisors. For example, at Talbot, Grunberg (1984) noted an increase in both the power and the span of supervision between 1977 and 1982. The important intervening event was the establishment of new working practices after the 1979 strike at Ryton. Ford UK sought to implement a new disciplinary procedure in 1979, and new work standards in 1980. Disputes at Halewood arose in 1980 around both issues but did not resolve the problem; again in 1981 and 1982 management suspended workers who could not meet new production standards and experienced strikes. Once more, BL experienced the most substantial changes. The assertion of the 'right to manage' in the autumn of 1979 went along with the publication of a document designed to disseminate a new managerial philosophy. 'Management at BL' opens: 'It is managers who have the responsibility for managing, leading and motivating employees and for communicating on company matters ... shop stewards have the right to represent and to communicate trade union information to their members at the workplace but only within the rules and procedures jointly established.'

The document continued to spell out the importance of the integrity of managerial hierarchy, the use of specific information channels for communicating with employees, and the need to defeat 'the small minority who would like to see BL fail'. Together with the removal of mutuality and the implementation of group working in which the foreman is the linchpin, it sought to re-establish the role of the first-line supervisor in production. At Vauxhall's Ellesmere Port plant a similar message was passed to management staff following the 1979 strike: 'It is essential that all employees start back to work knowing and accepting that we will manage. The message must be clear. It is only by us managing the business that Ellesmere Port will once again get back on the road to total success.'

WORKING PRACTICES

A report (IDS 1981) on changes in working practices broke the observed changes in British industry in general into four main types:

1. increased flexibility and mobility of labour often achieved by enforcing previously unenforced agreements;
2. self-inspection, workers being given additional responsibilities, specifically to reduce the need for inspectors;
3. tighter discipline and work standards, for example through stricter adherence to relaxation times and meal breaks, reducing systematic overtime, increasing direct supervision and work measurement;
4. speeding up, for example, through an increase of the pace of the line, or through multi-machine manning.

All of the types of changes in working discussed by IDS were attempted in the motor industry between 1979 and 1983, and all firms attempted to reform shop-floor working practices in the period 1979–83. Ford and Vauxhall relied on enforcing existing arrangements. For example, Ford's 1982 efficiency agreement is essentially a reaffirmation by senior trade union officials of their commitment to agreed principles for achieving efficiency, while a similar understanding followed the resolution of the 1979 strike at Vauxhall's Ellesmere Port plant. BL, on the other hand, effected changes in 1980 which completely altered the basis upon which working practices were established. Talbot's management, whilst not forced to change agreements as extensively as their equivalents at BL, did impose changes in the face of union opposition.

The key point at BL was the removal of 'mutuality'. This principle had required managers to agree changes with shop stewards in *advance* of implementation, and was incorporated in plant procedure agreements. The scope of mutual agreement varied between plants, but at both Longbridge and Cowley plants issues such as manning levels, setting of performance standards, relief allowances, and mobility were subject to those provisions.

The removal of mutuality depended on the implementation of the so-called 'Blue Newspaper' (draft November, 1979, Pay and Conditions Agreement) introduced in April, 1980. The document tidied up the agreements concerning centralized bargaining and the job evaluation system, formalized industrial engineering arrangements and established an incentive scheme, new working practices, and the right of management to determine unilaterally the range of items previously covered by mutuality. So whereas agreement previously had to precede change, following the Blue Newspaper, during arguments about work standards it was required that: 'The employee will continue to work to the prescribed method and the work standard or work assignment while the resolution procedure is in question.' The Blue Newspaper was not accepted by trade unions, but it was extremely important for managers. Edwardes has suggested that it led to inefficient work practices being 'thrown out of the window' (see p. 31 above).

The implementation of change was, however, more uneven than this: at Longbridge and several other plants in the Birmingham area working practices were reformed in 1980, but elsewhere, for example, Cowley Assembly plant, disputes over the terms of the Blue Newspaper took place as late as 1983 (see Chapter 6).

The collective agreements at Vauxhall, Talbot, and Ford had never inhibited flexibility of labour. However, there are some signs that the issue of flexibility became important in the early 1980s, which implies custom and practice did limit flexibility. This may have been because practice had departed from agreement, or because the amount of mobility required had increased. In any event, Ford sought the renewed efficiency commitment in 1982, and the 1984 Vauxhall agreement, which settled a two-week strike, offered a new wage structure in return for *inter alia* acceptance of broader jobs and enhanced mobility.

As might be expected, the greatest changes were at BL. For the mass of restrictive provisions on individual and gang mobility contained in plant-level direct and indirect agreements, the Blue Newspaper substituted the following: 'Any employee may be called upon to work in any part of his employing plant and/or to carry out any grade or category of work within the limits of his abilities and experience, with training if necessary.' Other elements of the document were important here. The job evaluation scheme condensed the previous 500 or so classifications of hourly paid employees into five company-wide grades. The incentive scheme put earnings in all plants on a similar output-related basis. Neither were accessible to negotiation by shop stewards at plant level.

But some of the more substantial changes at BL were not mentioned in the Blue Newspaper and in fact were planned prior to it. The two most important changes were the introduction of teamworking and the idea of two-trades response. The essential principle of teamworking is that operations within a given production zone should be organized around a single supervisor: within the team so formed there was to be little demarcation between the jobs of individual members, and rotation of certain tasks, including some routine maintenance. The team would be responsible for all aspects of production within a given area. This represented a substantial change from the then current practice in the company. Flexibility of labour between direct jobs was restricted both by the requirement to agree transfer with worker representatives and the terms of the various local agreements which specified a number of boundaries to mobility areas.

The proposed team organization is given in *Figure 5*. The team foreman's role was the linchpin, since under this format all resources required for production within the zone were to come under the foreman, and responsibility for output from the zone was to lie with him. Within the teams, it was proposed not only that a certain amount of job rotation would take place but also that progression from material handler to operator to quality controller to maintenance would be possible. The introduction of female workers on direct jobs was also considered.

Other support for the teams came from two areas. The on-line quality control function was to be audited by a specialist quality-control function, and the main support services were to remain under their own supervision. The team supervisor would still remain the first level of management, although it

Figure 5 Composition of production teams at BL

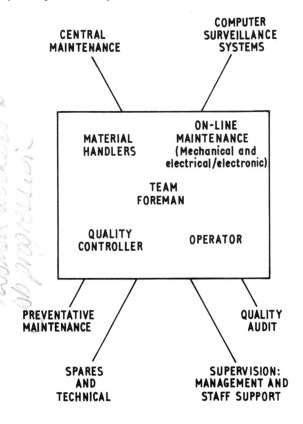

Source: Willman and Winch (1985).

was expected that their numbers would reduce as the need for supervision by trade disappeared (see below). Overall, management control over teamwork was to be facilitated by computer-based production monitoring systems.

The essence of the move to two-trades maintenance response was to be the removal of demarcation between different craft skills. In BL at the time maintenance workers were organized into a range of distinct trades such as fitters, millwrights, pipefitters, electricians, plumbers, and electronics engineers. All maintenance was organized centrally, and, in the event of malfunction, the appropriate trades were called out. The two-trades response is based on unreformed maintenance trades, as distinct from two-trades maintenance which is based on reformed training and apprenticeship arrangements.

BL wished to abolish trade demarcations and to create two trade groups: electrical and mechanical. It was not seen as feasible to go beyond this, since there was seen to be a deep divide between electrical and mechanical trades, and study of two-trades work systems at the Fiat Mirafiori plant, visited by members of the BL participation scheme had impressed both the company and trade union representatives.

However, a further and more radical change to maintenance was envisaged, which was the development of 'on-line' mainten-ance within production teams. As *Figure 5* illustrates, the teamwork approach was to place maintenance staff under non-specialist direct supervision. In fact, three tiers of maintenance were envisaged in a work system which tended to remove the distinction between direct and indirect work. These tiers were:

1. 'minor maintenance' tasks, such as initial fault diagnosis and coping with air and water leaks, which were to be performed by the operators within teams;
2. 'medium breakdowns' to be dealt with by an on-line maintenance crew whose responsibility extended to prevent-ative maintenance;
3. 'major breakdowns', requiring equipment replacement or manpower in excess of the on-line capacity or specialist knowledge, which would be dealt with by calling out a central maintenance crew.

The purpose of this division was to reduce lengthy response times to faults, the costs of which escalated once high-volume automated assembly techniques were adopted. For example, with volumes of around 4,500 per week, the Metro line produces over 55 body shells an hour so that relatively short periods of downtime can be very costly.

Of these two proposed changes, the second (on-line maintenance) was undoubtedly the most important. It was the most important because its benefits were clear-cut in terms of the calculated reduction in response times. By contrast, the benefits of teamworking were contested by a number of managers since lack of direct labour flexibility was not seen as a cause of major production losses, and job rotation raised the spectre of difficulties in quality assurance. Teamworking was the more far-reaching organizationally. Not only did it seek to change the craft organization of work, which was defended by unions on the basis of job security, it also, and in consequence, required major changes to the organization of lower management in the move away from functional supervision. This form of organization was at least partially rooted in demarcations within maintenance trades.

These developments at BL have been to some extent paralleled elsewhere. At Ford UK there has been considerable use of redeployment, one very good example being the movement of labour to the labour-intensive parts of assembly on the Sierra after it had been displaced from the more automated sections of the production line. In the USA, GM has implemented teamworking in several plants (Katz 1985).

'Self-inspection' along with 'self-maintenance' are to some extent catchwords, but they express an important idea. The training managers in the firms we interviewed reasoned that it would be largely uneconomical to provide all semi-skilled operators with all the skills needed to maintain their own machines. However, with existing demarcation rules, fairly rudimentary pieces of maintenance may require skilled labour. Nevertheless, at all four companies there are examples of operators doing simple maintenance work such as oiling, and elementary bits of materials handling. At BL this is associated with teamworking, and the blurring of distinctions between direct and indirect work. Attempts to encourage improved quality and self-inspection through making workers sign off their work were resisted in some of BL's plants, but by 1985 all operators were following this practice. At Ford, such changes are associated with the quality emphasis and the cost reduction of the 'After Japan' campaign, but attempts to initiate self-inspection have been rejected by the unions. At Vauxhall one of the commitments associated with the introduction of a new wage structure in 1984 was the acceptance by production operators of defect reporting and correction. At Talbot, the most significant redesign of jobs has been the merging of separate inspection and rectification jobs, the former an indirect job, the latter a direct.

The impetus for change in this area has come from the need to increase productivity, facilitated by new technology which has simplified a number of maintenance tasks, and improved quality to such an extent that in certain cases inspection is redundant or is automated. All firms have stressed the need to build 'right first time' and gauging and other self-inspection tasks are built into the work standard. Consequently increased manning levels are not likely to result from the changing nature of inspection.

The issue of effort intensity must be related to improvements in production methods. There are reports of people working harder, but this may not necessarily mean they arrive home very much more tired than they did, say, five years ago. The main difference in people's jobs reported by the stewards we interviewed is not the effort; rather it is that the time people are spending working may have increased, and more importantly their increased mobility between jobs. At the Cowley body shop, for example, there are reports of harder working, but this has to be qualified by the less arduous nature of most jobs: for example the parts are lighter, and people are not working nearly as hard and in such harsh conditions as they did under piecework.

The clearest information on the intensification of effort comes once more from BL, and is based on discussions surrounding the use of industrial engineering data. The intention of the Blue Newspaper was to secure access for industrial engineers to set standard times and manning levels on the basis of effort expenditure at 100 per cent BSI. Although industrial engineering was used before the Blue Newspaper, this document standardized arrangements by formalizing management's right to use various industrial engineering techniques. More importantly, the ending of mutuality removed the necessity for standards to be agreed before they could be implemented. This in itself was seen by industrial engineers as an opportunity to remove 'slack' previously introduced through mutuality, and they hold the view that between 1980 and 1983 much of this slack was removed. Moreover, in 1981, the company sought to absorb the costs of a reduction in the working week from 40 to 39 hours both by reducing relaxation time and by setting manning assignments around a target of 101.5 per cent BSI on direct work. Given the absence of accurate effort standard data, it is almost impossible to compare these effort levels with those under piecework in the 1960s. However, it seems reasonable to conclude that the effort levels set by industrial engineers in Austin Rover after 1980 caused effort intensification − at least on direct work − in comparison with the standards of the late 1970s.

Such changes to effort levels were not confined to BL. Line speeds and output increased at Talbot's Ryton plant after the 1979 dispute. Such a finding would not be remarkable at BL or Ford, given the role of new process layout and automation in assisting speed-up. At Talbot, however, there was little new investment in production equipment. The issue of reduction of relaxation time is, in fact, closely related to this, both in terms of management intent and timing of implementation. Comparison of Ryton and Poissy from the mid-1970s to 1983 shows that while rest allowances actually increased in the French plant, at Ryton they decreased from 10.5 per cent to 9.5 per cent of working time across the same period (Grunberg 1984). Ford and Vauxhall had never allowed local bargaining about rest periods, and experienced relatively few problems.

At BL, these changes to effort levels followed the introduction of 'Blue Newspaper' practices. At Longbridge in 1980 and 1981 local 'togging up' and tea-break arrangements were progressively removed, but only after strike action. Subsequently, throughout BL, accommodation to the 39-hour week involved the introduction of manning arrangements geared to a personal relaxation time of 10 per cent (rather than the previous 11 per cent) on direct work, and 9.5 per cent on indirect work. In some plants, however, this left local arrangements unchanged, the most important of these being the three-minute early finishing allowance at Cowley Body and Assembly plant, which was only removed after a sizeable dispute in 1983 (see Chapter 6).

Overall, the reform of working practices has been most

radical in BL: new managerial philosophies, new collective agreements, and new process efficiency requirements have come together in the period since 1980 to alter completely the basis upon which working practices are established. Nevertheless there has been change in all of the companies, including the managerial approaches to the implementation of change, and it is necessary to locate working practices in the wider industrial relations strategies.

CHANGES IN THE PROCEDURES REGULATING WORKING PRACTICES

Starting from different positions in the 1970s, the degree of reform in industrial relations has varied between firms. BL, which had piecework and plant bargaining, attempted considerable change in the 1970s. In a climate of crisis and with the worst industrial relations record in the industry, the management has made further changes in the late 1970s and early 1980s. For example, the number of full-time shop stewards at BL has been reduced from 20 to 6 in the first years of this decade; the range of issues over which they can bargain has also narrowed. The management originally imposed, and then later claimed to have gained agreement through the 1980 pay negotiations, for the Blue Newspaper changes to bargaining, pay, employee benefits, and productivity. Although this document remains a draft agreement, and the unions continue to contest its status, management treat it as an agreement and the basis on which they can implement changes in plants. Of special importance is the section on flexibility which aimed to ensure 'that there will be full co-operation in the movement of the labour to ensure the efficient continuity of production'.

At Talbot, in the 1970s, the existence of mutuality was also contested. The unions claimed they had the right to mutuality, and the stewards were able to frustrate attempts to move labour, particularly on a daily basis, and to inhibit management from taking initiatives. The key event following the introduction of an incentive scheme in 1978 was in 1979, when the stewards implicitly accepted an increased output level without any corresponding increase in labour. The 1981 agreement on industrial engineering introduced by management effectively consolidated existing practices, restated managerial policies, and introduced the right of management to vary line speeds. Ford and Vauxhall, never having had plant bargaining and piecework (although Vauxhall did have full-time stewards in some of their plants), did not have to reform industrial relations as dramatically as BL or Talbot. At Vauxhall the crucial change occurred after the 1979 strike at Ellesmere Port when, in the view of management, the power of the shop stewards had reached unmanageable proportions for management. The emphasis in the 1980s in both firms has been more on enforcing existing agreements than on creating new ones.

Although BL was distinctive in the severity of its crisis, managers at Ford and Vauxhall have displayed similar concerns with efficiency which similarly imply industrial relations changes. Yet the changes did not need to be as great, partly because of the existence of different agreements. For example, the long-standing agreement on job mobility at Vauxhall runs:

'Continuity of employment, as a feature of Company personnel policy, requires full acceptance of the principle of mobility of labour. It should be noted that the terms of the engagement letter require employees to accept transfer to work for which they may not have been specifically engaged.

'This mobility must exist in particular to correct imbalances in the production flow caused by such factors as machine, track or services breakdowns, shortage of materials or components, inordinately high absenteeism or absence on scheduled shifts, curtailment or elimination of particular production operations.'

Operating Manual, section 4, paragraph 6 (Associated with 1971 Pay Agreement)

It cannot be assumed that all such agreements were enforced or that practice invariably followed them. But, in some cases, increased mobility of labour of the kind which has been demanded, particularly at BL, was not necessary. Many of the changes in BL have involved movements between shifts and plants within the same site, when previously no such movement was possible. Similarly at the other companies, the increasing demand for mobility and other efficiency measures has called for greater use and clarification of existing agreements.

Procedures and institutions

By 1980, the major manufacturers had all achieved company level procedures for the negotiation of pay and the resolution of disputes. In an industry famed in the past for the bargaining power of shop-floor representatives, the reform of bargaining at BL terminated the capacity of shop stewards in the industry to bargain locally about pay. Another point of similarity is that all companies bargain at the company level jointly with representatives of all manual unions, and a third is that all have sought to institutionalize the division between negotiation at company level and consultation within the plants. At BL, the changing views about the frequency, scope, and location of bargaining came across in negotiations about the 'Blue Newspaper' in 1979. The company's rejoinder to the union claim for retention of mutuality at plant level ran as follows:

'The National Agreements and the old piecework agreements refer to mutual arrangements being come to between representatives of the workpeople and representatives of the employees on how piecework prices or terms are to be determined. We really are not in that scene ... we are sitting across from you as the representative body representing 90,000 odd people in BL Cars, and we are only seeking to come to a mutual arrangement with you as to how we operate. As we see it, that satisfies the principle you call "mutuality".'   Leyland Cars JNC Minutes 14:12:79

Such institutional changes affect the ways in which shop stewards operate. In all companies there is a formal recognized role for the shop stewards in the basic industrial engineering procedure; they will be involved at various stages of the work measurement procedure, attend industrial engineering appreciation courses, and get involved in any problems with work standards and assignments via the appropriate procedure. Despite institutional similarities, once more differences appear between firms. At Ford, the level of facilities given to shop stewards has not formally changed, and the level of their involvement in local day-to-day issues has not been markedly reduced. The decrease in the number employed has not been matched by a corresponding decrease in the number of recognized union representatives. Elsewhere change appears to have been more thorough-going: at Vauxhall, the mobility of shop stewards and the ease with which they can leave their jobs has in practice been considerably reduced; at Talbot, numbers of stewards and the span of their functions have both decreased such that from a position whereby 60 per cent of stewards on each shift were full-time at the Ryton plant, now only the two convenors are full-time.

Once more, BL needs to be dealt with separately, primarily because of the sheer scale of change in steward influence. In 1978, senior stewards were involved in participation arrangements which yielded some influence on the company's decisions about future strategy, but by 1980 relations between stewards and managers in the company had been substantially changed. The effects of this change on shop steward organization were considerable, although there were differences between plants.

The appropriate starting point for discussing changes on shop steward organization at BL is probably the dismissal, in 1979, of Derek Robinson, the Longbridge convenor. Centralization of bargaining, the withdrawal of a range of steward facilities, refusal to provide such facilities on the new Metro line, and the process of selection of personnel for the new line all served to alter the power of steward organization in 1980. However, at Longbridge an organization survived, and in 1982 stewards felt that they were in some ways a 'fitter' organization through having withstood changes designed to diminish their influence.

The events at Cowley assembly plant were similar in some respects. But here, the dismissal of a key activist in 1982 followed a reduction in the number of stewards and the use of more specific release procedures to allow stewards away from their places of work; once more, transfer of labour to new production facilities disrupted existing constituencies of representation. However, whereas at Longbridge the changes were eventually followed by a period of apparently stable labour relations, Cowley assembly plant appeared to experience a deterioration in manager–steward relationships not only up to the early finishing dispute of spring, 1983, but also thereafter. Although the company has sought to agree constituencies with the trade unions, there has never been agreement. In autumn, 1983, the TGWU claimed 52 per cent of constituencies had no electoral nominees and very few steward elections needed to be held. Stoppages occurred in 1984 over the unavailability of stewards to deal with grievances, during one of which the company complained that senior stewards had little control over sectional action by work groups.

Full discussion of the differences between these disputes here must await the analysis of the early finishing dispute in the next chapter, but it appears that some of the difficulties Cowley assembly plant management experienced in 1983 came from the breakdown in shop-floor organization. The company had never sought to secure such a breakdown, and had instead wanted to establish 'constitutional' trade unionism, the basis of which was to be the 1982 procedure, which re-established the relationship between company and unions on a new basis. An important element of this new relationship was the establishment of consultative – rather than participative – machinery at plant level. In this, BL were falling in line with more general trends in the industry.

Consultation and involvement

The use of consultation and direct communication has been increasing in all the major car firms. Firms have increasingly used news sheets and information bulletins as well as briefing sessions and consultative methods such as quality circles. (The circulation of 'The Future of Halewood' document mentioned earlier is a good example of this.) There is considerable emphasis in all companies on employee involvement, especially as this is allied to increasing the quality of production. Vauxhall has developed both a set of quality standards and a system for monitoring and publicizing them. Jaguar has implemented quality circles, with some success, while elsewhere in BL the 1982 procedure has been invoked to establish 'plant level committees' which are based on existing representative patterns and designed as forums for information dissemination. Where teamworking operates (mainly at Longbridge and Cowley) it is envisaged that teams will form the basic units of employee involvement in matters of quality and efficiency.

Quality circles and other such participative schemes may be viewed as attempts to increase identification with the firm and harness workers' commitment to corporate objectives. Several managers reported how during various disputes or production problems workers had come up with important suggestions or had said, 'Why don't you listen to us?' Yet there are dangers in exaggerating the importance of this kind of working knowledge, and certainly its existence cannot be seen as necessarily contributing to an involvement with the firm. It was impossible for us to ascertain whether workers have responded to the managements' strategies as intended, for example through accepting that their jobs can be made more secure by their increasing their commitment to the firm. A passive acceptance of change might be the simplest and most accurate way of summing up the situation.

The formal response to quality circles and other briefing methods by the trade unions has been negative. Ford, for example, has tried to discuss 'employee involvement' at the national level but has met with blanket rejection from the blue-collar unions, there as well as at the local level. It has, however, managed to gain acceptance and sign an agreement at the national level on the white-collar side. Opposition among the manual unions arises because such schemes are seen as management's attempt to bypass the formal trade union channels.

The 'After Japan' campaign at Ford initiated in 1979 was essentially a process of giving publicity to the need to face up to the competition. As such it sought to encourage employee involvement. The main focus at Ford has been on changing attitudes, the intention being to get what Bob Ramsey, former director of industrial relations of Ford Britain, called 'the real breakthrough in attitudes' that management felt they needed in order to compete, that is having 'given the unions more strength and greater security' by granting exclusive bargaining rights, automatic 'check-off' of union dues by the employer, a blue-collar agreement (a union membership agreement – authors' addition), and better facilities for shop stewards, for example. Ford have not managed to implement quality circles throughout their UK operations, although they do operate in some activities, such as the parts division at Daventry. However, quality circles are not central to the overall approach, which extends to a general commitment to better employee communication.

BL has had some success in one or two plants, and in Jaguar the convenor had accepted them to such an extent that he was used by BL management to speak publicly about them, both within and outside the company. Austin Rover, however, hold regular supervisors' zone meetings in which the issues discussed include quality problems but are by no means confined to them. At Vauxhall the convenor and senior shop steward have rejected all attempts at such consultative arrangements, preferring to argue that the existing monthly joint consultative body is sufficient; but they allow departmental stewards the discretion as to whether to co-operate or not. A further example of this division between the two sides can be seen in the outcome of the 1983 Vauxhall agreement, in which a joint productivity committee was set up. But by the start of the next round of negotiations, summer, 1984, it had met only once and had widened the discussion to include job security and structure as well as work practices. Talbot having met with resistance to quality circles – partly on the grounds that it is management's job to manage – has largely confined its initiatives to regular briefing sessions between supervisors and their work groups, which are often preceded by video films showing, for example, dealer comments on quality and customer reaction.

These developments in employee involvement and consultation relate to the discussion of the role of the shop stewards. The emphasis in the recent strategy of all four companies has not been on fundamentally changing the method of industrial relations, through, for example, dismantling the shop steward structure. Rather it has been based on developing systems of joint consultation and employee involvement that are allied to the existing system of collective bargaining and aimed at encouraging increased productivity and understanding of the commercial problems confronting the company. The stewards' power and sphere of influence may be weakened, but they may remain an integral part of the representative and managerial system. Many of the changes in working practices, and certainly the overall structure which has facilitated specific changes, have been introduced through collective bargaining or are covered by previous agreements. The chief exception was BL where the crucial changes were implemented by the company after management had first put them directly to the employees. BL's management in the late 1970s attempted to bypass the union structure through the use of ballots, seeking acquiescence to certain changes, and then pressing ahead with them, where they did not gain a majority in support for their initiatives.

Incentives and pay

By 1981, Ford stood out as the only company which did not rely on output-based incentives for a proportion of pay. BL, Talbot, and Vauxhall all operated essentially non-negotiable output-based incentive schemes. These differed substantially from the old piecework arrangements which once were common in the industry, although they similarly exposed manual employees to the effects of product-market fluctuations in their earnings in a way that the Ford system still does not. Ford operates an attendance bonus which does not relate to output.

The largest bonus components, and thus the greatest potential for earnings variation, are at Vauxhall and BL, both of which experienced disputes during 1984 over bonus variation. The relationship between basic pay levels and bonus differs between companies. At annual pay negotiations, Ford and Vauxhall have usually looked for agreements on changed working practices in return for pay rises as, for example, in the autumn of 1984, when the Vauxhall deal gave an extra 1 per cent for acceptance of redeployment arrangements. In contrast, BL has sought to use the bonus scheme to secure changes in working practices, particularly in the acceptance of change and the reduction of indirect work, and to consolidate bonus at the annual or biennial review as part of the pay deal. Since consolidation raises the efficiency level at which a given bonus is earned, the scheme, according to one manager, 'moves the goalposts back' and reinforces efficiency improvements. At Talbot, the main point that management stress is that with high increases in efficiency there has to be consolidation to avoid making more than about 15 per cent of the wage packet subject to output fluctuations.

The promise of job security and the 'After Japan' campaign

The negative incentive, the fear of unemployment, has been an important component of the change of strategy of all four companies. Supervisors responding to workers with phrases such as 'If you don't like it you know what you can do', and similar kinds of behaviour were reported to lie behind the several complaints of excessive swearing by supervisors at the time of the bell-to-bell dispute at Cowley in 1983. Furthermore, increased use of the disciplinary procedure has been reported in all firms, although as the shadow of unemployment has hung around the shop floor in the 1980s managers have not necessarily had to be so explicit. Furthermore, in negotiations around plant closures and manpower reductions, as well as the annual wage negotiations, the threat of further redundancies has been made throughout the car industry. Yet managers have tried to turn this into a positive message: there will be increased job security for those remaining if there is compliance with job loss and acceptance of new working practices.

Similarly, the threat of foreign competition has been presented in a positive light, as a challenge to be met with skill and initiative at all levels of the organization. All firms have personalized the threat, in the form of Japanese competition. Japan, as the major competitor to be fought in the market-place, is the provider of ideas and productivity targets which must be met in order for British industry to survive. Exhortations to improve quality and productivity through the 'right first time' mentality have gone right down the line. Ford has been most explicit in this respect with what it called an 'After Japan' campaign, but such exercises are more than simply exhortations backed up by posters in work-places or briefing meetings. In Ford's case it began with managers being sent to Japan to see, in the words of one senior manager, 'exactly what they were up against'. The lessons to be learned from these and other exercises both in Ford and elsewhere were essentially about production methods. As such the 'After Japan' campaign has been largely an engineering, and to a lesser extent an accounting, exercise. It has involved the attempt to reduce inventories and complexity in manufacture, and to reduce the time taken to change tools. The need to integrate trades and change working practices had already been acknowledged although the Japanese experience further fuelled the urgency with which management felt they should pursue this.

In short, After Japan has been more about reducing inventories and 'right first time' production than about a new form of work commitment and industrial relations. The changes which Ford and other managements have pursued in the light of the Japanese approach were both aimed at and the result of improving managerial competence. This has implications for the firms' industrial relations strategy, for their managements have attempted to use the improvements in management as leverage in their attempts to increase commitment and persuade workers to accept change. In this way managerial competence is being used as an attempt to legitimize managerial authority. However, managements are sceptical of the extent to which the 'lesson has got through' and still detect antagonistic attitudes and what they call 'the ritual of confrontation'.

CONCLUSIONS

This chapter has concentrated on the changes in working practices and industrial relations which have occurred in the car industry. It is a story of evolution and not revolution, as one manager we interviewed put it. Much of what has been done has been, to quote from the same manager, 'carrying out what management felt should have been done in the past' and consequently managers have concentrated on regaining initiatives that they had 'given away in the past', a phrase which is very much in currency amongst the managers we interviewed.

In this chapter we have examined the changes in industrial methods and working practices which lie behind the reductions in manning levels and increased productivity. The role these have played within the considerable improvements in the industry's position remains a matter of controversy, and cannot be precisely calculated.

In making changes each firm has been aiming towards achieving West German standards. Nevertheless, there has been a concern about Japanese methods. Particularly important has been the attempt to learn from their systems of production and stock control. BL has been especially able to benefit from its co-operation with Honda. Yet there has been no major attempt to copy the Japanese system of labour relations, and there is scepticism amongst both management and unions about the feasibility or desirability of this approach. Where quality circles have been used they have been adapted to the local situation. Increasing the flexibility of workers has less to do with imitating Japan than with the need to improve productivity and maintain production levels with much reduced work-forces and the effects of the changing technology. As we saw in the previous chapter there is little evidence to suggest that such changes will affect the relative importance of internal and external recruitment. There is no commitment to recruitment through only one, or a limited number, of entry points. Even the changes in training associated with multi-skilled work are unlikely to alter the reliance on local labour markets – since even the new skill combinations consist of a high component of transferable skills. Yet the changes, as well as the high rate of unemployment, may increase the stability of much of the work-force.

Whilst the managerial strategies of the four companies have consisted of many common elements, it is important not to draw the conclusion that they are all following identical paths. Whilst they do operate in the same industrial relations context, and have a common problem, competition – and it is certainly not the so-called excess capacity of the industry – they are working from different starting points and with different resources.

There is some evidence of a new style of management, although its precise nature is not clear. Important features are the increasing sophistication in industrial engineering, itself facilitated by increasing computerization, the ending of mutuality at BL, improvements within management, and the re-emphasis of management's right to manage. However, to label it simply as 'macho-management' would be to ignore other changes such as group working, quality circles, moves to increase employee involvement and consultation, and above all the large number of organizational changes which have increased efficiency.

There is then a multi-dimensional nature to the managerial strategies which includes the role of bargaining in the implementation of the changes, the improvement of management quality and organization, and the attempts to improve job design and the total remuneration package. At the risk of some over-simplification, one can characterize the strategy behind industrial relations reform as an attempt to minimize the extent to which employees and their representatives could interfere with production efficiency while maximizing their commitment to efficiency as a desirable goal. As the next chapter will show, the success of such strategies has been mixed.

Within the terms of Katz and Streeck (1984) this is perhaps best characterized as a 'co-operative strategy', strongly influenced by events in the USA (the success of Employee Involvement and concession bargaining) and Japanese management methods, but operating in a 'neo-liberal' context with long-standing institutions and resistance from trade unions. Certainly, all managements stress that their strategy is not so much to avoid bargaining, or an outright rejection of it, but rather is aimed at changing the scope of bargaining in management's favour.

SIX
STRIKES

INTRODUCTION

The avoidance of strikes has become a high priority for the car firms particularly because the improvements in efficiency and investment in automated assembly techniques have raised rates of output thus increasing the cost of unnecessary downtime. For competitive reasons, it is important that car firms do not lose sales through strikes. Nevertheless, the industry still has a relatively high level of strike activity. In 1973, working days lost per thousand workers in the car industry was 12.6 times that for all industries and services, and in 1983 it was 9.8 times greater.[1] Throughout the post-war period in fact the motor industry has experienced a relatively high level of industrial conflict, and its industrial relations have attracted a good deal of public attention and criticism.

Strike activity in the UK car industry has been the subject of two detailed studies. The first, which greatly influenced the Donovan Commission, was that of Turner, Clack, and Roberts (1967); the second was that of Durcan, McCarthy, and Redman (1983). The first covers the post-war period to 1964 and the latter to 1973, but neither have focused on the UK industry in the period of adjustment since the first oil crisis.

This chapter focuses on the period 1973–84, but first it describes the two earlier studies. Second, it examines data on the pattern of strike activity since 1973. This data is of two types: official statistics on conflict in the industry, and the manufacturer's own figures on working time lost. It will be argued that the pattern of conflict between 1979 and 1983 differs markedly from that of earlier periods in focusing on job rights rather than pay to a greater extent than in the past. This follows from the changes in labour utilization patterns described above, which in turn can be related to changing product market conditions and production technology. One consequence of the changes is that the current pattern of conflict experienced by different manufacturers is similar. This similarity extends to the re-emergence of pay conflict in 1984.

EXPLANATIONS OF CONFLICT BEFORE 1973

Turner, Clack, and Roberts (1967) explained strike activity up to 1964 by the instability of both earnings and of employment. They pointed first to the cyclical and seasonal employment variations which resulted from changing production requirements and second to high but unstable earnings which varied both over time and between groups as major contributory factors to the pattern of strikes in the industry. Both forms of instability were seen to be the result of severe fluctuations in product demand, and they suggest: 'A large part of the car firm's high strike incidence ... has apparently represented the industry's substitute for a formally agreed means of dealing with recurrent labour surplus' (p. 332). They observed that working days lost tended to rise during recession and suggested that negotiators on both sides saw strike activity as a means of reducing output to avoid lay-offs.

Turner, Clack, and Roberts argued that these factors worked through workers' expectations, and they identified two important sets:

1. An expectation of 'fair wages': that earnings should be fair relative to those of similar jobs elsewhere, and in comparison with the employee's past experience. The logical extension of this is that work loads should be negotiable, 'since it would be meaningless to insist that earnings should be "fair"

in comparative terms without requiring that efforts, too, be regulated by agreeably comparative standards' (1967: 337).

2. An expectation of a 'job property' right: i.e. not only an expectation of continued employment with a particular company, but also the right to a particular job at a particular location.

Turner, Clack, and Roberts also suggested that a further contributory factor might be an 'obsolescence in the institutions' arising from the failure of the EEF-CSEU procedural arrangements to accommodate workers' expectations (1967: 339–44).

Durcan, McCarthy, and Redman (1983) cover the additional years between 1964 and 1973 when strike levels were much higher than those noted by Turner, Clack, and Roberts. As

Table 8 *Strike activity in motor vehicles 1949–83*

period	average number of strikes per annum	average working days lost per year (000s)
1949–53	25.4	170.4
1954–58	35.4	125.6
1959–63	106.2	377.6
1964–68	185.6	544.0
1969–73	272.6	1,853.2
1974–78	194.0	1,893.6
1979–83	105.2	1,069.0

Source: Durcan, McCarthy, and Redman (1983); DE Gazette, July 1974–July 1984.

Notes: Statistical basis as follows: 1949–59, 1948 SIC, MLH 80; 1960–69, 1958 SIC, MLH 381; 1970–82, 1968 SIC, MLH 381; 1983, 1980 SIC, MLH 351.

Table 8 shows, on several different measures, the level of conflict in the industry rose markedly after 1963 and spectacularly after 1968. During this latter period several of the sources of the earlier earnings and employment instability had been removed – notably piecework and the lack of redundancy protection. In particular Durcan, McCarthy, and Redman stress the hardening of product markets and a long-term loss of international competitiveness, and argue that Turner, Clack, and Roberts lay too great an emphasis on the notion of 'institutional obsolescence'.

The general picture of strike activity in the car industry since 1973 shows escalating conflict to 1979, and a somewhat reduced level thereafter. This pattern is described more fully below.

STRIKE ACTIVITY 1974–83

The industry experienced a higher level of strike activity in the 1970s than the 1960s (*Tables 8* and 9). Durcan, McCarthy, and

Table 9 *Strike activity, car industry 1974–83*

year	no. strikes	no. working days lost (000s)	no. working days lost per 000 workers	no. of workers involved[a]	
				000s	as % of employees[b]
1974	223	1,752	3,534	94.4	19.1
1975	150	824	1,814	61.1	13.7
1976	191	785	1,751	76.6	17.0
1977	212	2,745	5,611	95.1	22.4
1978	194	3,362	7,416	124.4	25.9
1979	165	3,064	6,700	285.3	62.4
1980	92	436	1,027	50.4	12.5
1981	136	749	2,158	124.2	37.9
1982	143	551	1,795	131.8	44.0
1983	90	545	1,760	69.6	23.0

Source: DE Gazette.
Notes:
a Figures refer to direct involvement.
b Quarterly estimates, September each year. 1983 figures refer to MLH 35.

Redman (1983) place the beginning of the upsurge of industrial conflict in the motor industry in 1969. Between 1974 and 1983, the number of working days lost peaked in the period 1977–79, as the industry experienced several large pay disputes. Nevertheless, in terms of the number of employees affected by strike action, conflict remained widespread in 1979 and 1981–82. We shall discuss the factors underlying this below.

Although working days lost between 1980 and 1983 were lower than in the 1970s, the incidence of conflict remained high. Much of the reduction in total days lost was a consequence of the industry's severe employment loss. The number of strikes and working days lost per thousand workers remains much higher in the car industry than the national average (*Table 10*).

Table 10 *Relative incidence of strikes and of strikes over pay, motor vehicles*

year	incidence of strikes		percentage of strikes over pay issues			
	ratio motor vehicles to all industries and services		all industries		motor vehicles	
	working days lost per 1,000 workers	no. strikes per 1,000 workers	strikes	working days lost	strikes	working days lost
1974	5.5	3.5	65.8	88.3	60.5	74.7
1975	6.9	3.4	57.8	75.2	53.3	68.2
1976	12.0	4.7	43.4	52.2	47.0	61.0
1977	12.5	4.2	57.6	79.2	55.7	68.2
1978	18.0	3.8	61.1	78.9	51.1	82.4
1979	5.3	4.0	59.1	93.4	53.3	87.0
1980	2.0	3.8	47.7	88.6	39.1	60.1
1981	11.0	6.8	46.9	62.0	27.9	43.8
1982	7.1	6.9	42.8	66.3	30.1	24.0
1983	9.8	4.7	40.5	58.1	25.6	20.6

Source: DE Gazette.

Notes: Motor vehicles employment base as *Table 8*. National rates per 1,000 on basis of 'employees in employment', September each year.

Strike trends in the industry have not followed those nationally. Whereas 1980 was a turning point in the reduction of strike activity nationally, it was not so in the car industry. Strikes in the industry also had different causes (*Table 10*). Between 1974 and 1983, the share of disputes over pay in the total has decreased far more rapidly in the car industry than elsewhere, a trend visible in both the series on working days lost and on numbers of strikes, and particularly marked since

1980. Between 1981 and 1983, when the percentage of pay stoppages was historically low, other principal causes of stoppages and of working days lost in the industry were respectively: manning and work allocation 28.7 per cent and 17.8 per cent; dismissal 18.7 per cent and 20.3 per cent; working practices and supervision 8.9 per cent and 2.4 per cent; duration and scheduling of hours of work 5.4 per cent and 10.0 per cent; and redundancy 4.8 per cent and 16.7 per cent. Whereas the first three prompted small strikes (they account for a higher percentage of strikes than of working days lost), disputes over working time and redundancy tended to be larger.

To summarize, in the car industry the level of strike activity remained high between 1974 and 1983. The fall in overall working days lost is accounted for primarily by employment loss, but both the number of strikes and working days lost per thousand workers remained high in the early 1980s. Two peaks of activity are evident, from 1977–79 and 1981–83. Whereas the first is characterized by large pay stoppages and high levels of working days lost the second is characterized by non-pay issues and the involvement of a relatively high percentage of the work-force.

EXPLAINING THE PATTERN

By 1974, many of the institutional features to which Turner, Clack, and Roberts had attributed the industry's strike pattern had changed. The indigenous manufacturers had merged into BLMC, and piecework payment on production had been largely removed by the implementation of measured day-work. By 1980, with the centralization of bargaining at BL, the four main manufacturers had removed the possibility of fair wage claims based on anomalies produced by fragmented collective bargaining. It might be expected, therefore, that 'job rights' or 'fair work load' issues might become more important. Second, because there are now substantially fewer car assembly operations the strike performance of particular firms and plants should exert greater influence over the performance of the industry as a whole. In fact, as we shall show, both of these trends are observable.

Two points stand out. First, there was no large-scale dispute over pay between 1979 and 1983 (*Table 11*) despite the fact that centralization of bargaining at BL had removed small pay

Table 11 *Large strikes in the car industry 1974–83*

year	month	manufacturer	size	issue
1974	Apr.	BL	110,300	lay-off protest
	Aug.	Leyland Vehicles	129,400	pay
	Aug./Sept.	Ford	132,200	washing up time
	Sept./Oct.	Ford	143,700	shift allowances
	Nov./Dec.	BL	141,400	lay-off pay
1975	Apr./June	Ford	115,500	manning levels
	May/June	Chrysler	116,400	pay
1976				
1977	Feb./Mar.	BL	454,000	tool-room dispute
	June	Ford	123,400	lay-off pay
	Oct./Nov.	Vauxhall	485,600	differentials
	Nov./Feb.	BL	282,900	manning levels
1978	Jan./Feb.	Ford	245,700	new working practices
	Aug./Sept.	Leyland Vehicles	139,400	pay
	Sept./Nov.	Ford	2,500,000	pay
1979	July/Oct.	Talbot	300,000	pay
	Aug./Sept.	Vauxhall	315,600	pay
	Nov.	BL	189,900	Robinson dismissal
1980	Apr.	BL	173,600	Blue Newspaper
1981	Jan./Feb.	Ford	161,600	subcontracting of work
	May	Ford	103,000	discipline
	Nov./Dec.	BL	148,300	rest allowances
1982	Jan./Feb.	Leyland Vehicles	247,900	redundancy
1983	Mar./Apr.	Ford	190,000	'Kelly' dispute
	Mar./Apr.	BL	125,700	'washing up' dispute

Source: DE Gazette.

bargaining units. Second, the large stoppages are dominated by events at Ford and BL, especially since 1979, as employment at Talbot and Vauxhall has fallen.

The pay issue is of particular interest because of changes affecting the system of pay determination at BL and the decline of car workers' pay relative to other industries. Such comparisons may have been important in pay bargaining: for example, they have featured in the comprehensive claims submitted by the TGWU to Ford. However, as Turner, Clack, and Roberts (1967) show, comparisons *within* the industry were more salient, at least in the 1960s when company level bargaining was less common. Even in Ford, the issue of parity with Leyland generated substantial conflict in the early 1970s (Beynon 1973: 289–316).

These two sets of comparisons feature in the explanation of the rise in strike activity in 1977–79. As *Table 11* shows, the *largest* disputes during the period were about pay. The tool-room dispute at BL and that at Vauxhall in October, 1977, concerned differentials: over the next two years, four large disputes at Ford, Vauxhall, Chrysler, and Leyland Vehicles concerned the annual pay review. BL Cars is conspicuous in its avoidance of large pay disputes during this period, primarily because the parity programme which established a single bargaining unit was not fully completed until April, 1980 (Willman and Winch 1985). This was because earnings increases at BL Cars during the period were substantially greater than those at the other three main manufacturers. The changes at BL were seen to be funded by productivity increases during bargaining reform, and so, in effect, they were exempt from the incomes policy constraints to which other companies were subject.

In the retooling phase after 1980, the focus of large stoppages shifts from remuneration to effort levels and their enforcement. As we have shown in Chapter 3, work-pace and working practices changed in rather different ways and to rather different extents across the industry. Nevertheless, the parallels between companies, particularly Ford and BL, in terms of strike activity are worth considering.

Within BL, the relationship between changing working practices, retooling, and strike activity is particularly clear-cut.

After the imposition of the 'Blue Newspaper' in April, 1980, the largest disputes within the company occurred at Longbridge where the Metro was to be launched in October. Between April and the end of the year, a number of disputes took place over issues such as rest allowances, production targets, and discipline. In 1981, although the company experienced a pay dispute over the November annual review, Longbridge experienced a far greater loss of working time in disputes over production targets and rest allowances; in particular, the implementation of a 39-hour week without production loss caused a large dispute in November about the reduction of rest allowances (Willman and Winch 1985). But this level of conflict was short-lived. Large disputes at Longbridge accounted for 20.5 per cent of recorded working days lost in motor vehicles in 1980, and 25.7 per cent in 1981, but no large stoppages are recorded at the plant in 1982 and the percentage for 1983 is 2.6 per cent.

By 1983, conflict around the implementation of the Blue Newspaper had switched to Cowley, where the Maestro was launched in March. However, the link to events at Longbridge is fairly direct. In November, 1981, rest allowance reductions had been proposed at Cowley as at Longbridge, and in the assembly plant, failing agreement, shorter allowances were imposed in February, 1982, according to the 'Longbridge formula'. However, whereas at Longbridge 'togging up' allowances[2] had been eradicated before the Metro launch, the practice of 'early finishing' had persisted at Cowley. The parallel practice of allowing three minutes 'washing up' time also remained at the body plant. From the company's perspective, the pressures to maximize capacity utilization increased markedly with the Maestro launch. With a line speed of 37 cars per hour, the extra hour provided by eradication of early finishing (on a two-shift system) would allow production of an extra 1,700 cars per year.[3] From the employees' point of view it represented a further increase in work-pace, since rest allowances were to be further reduced. Moreover, although the TGWU stressed that they did not seek to overturn the April, 1980, changes, the terms of the Blue Newspaper upon which the company's action was predicated had never been agreed. The dispute over the issue lasted from 28 March to 26 April, although disagreement continued after the return to work and 'bell-to-bell' working was only established in July. The terms of the return to work included the establishment of a joint inquiry team to investigate industrial relations in the assembly plant.

The team's report illustrated the complexity of the issues underlying the dispute. It noted that employees complained that the degree of mobility required was excessive, that they were required to work too hard, that supervisors were guilty of abusive behaviour, that health and safety and 'housekeeping' issues received insufficient managerial attention, and that trade union facilities were inadequate. On the other hand, plant management complained that trade unions did not accept the need to be competitive, that the structure of trade union organization in the assembly plant was poor, that unions sought to use health and safety issues as a bargaining counter, and that employees 'stop work too often'.

The recommendations of the team covered all these issues, but the problems in the plant were not immediately resolved. A change in plant management occurred, and the managers tended to diagnose the dispute as resulting from too much change too quickly. But shop stewards in the plant voted to strike once more in June if bell-to-bell working were imposed; and when such working was imposed on the Maestro line in July, after rejection of the strike call, it was not on the basis of agreement. Overall, in 1983, strikes at Cowley accounted for 24 per cent of recorded working days lost in the industry.

While Cowley succeeded Longbridge as BL's problem area, the Halewood plant had long been seen by Ford management as its problem plant in the UK. The company's own figures show that the plant accounted for a disproportionate fraction of UK hours and sales losses between 1978 and 1982 (*Figure 6*). Although retooling had assisted a reduction in labour and overhead costs of 6.2 per cent in 1981 and 7.2 per cent in 1982, similar improvements in continental plants left the productivity differential intact. Failure to achieve self-certification of work, on-line maintenance, operator maintenance, and the removal of a range of demarcations on direct work left Halewood well down on several efficiency measures in 1983. Despite the efficiency agreements in the 'After Japan' package presented to the unions in 1981, management found shop-floor practices

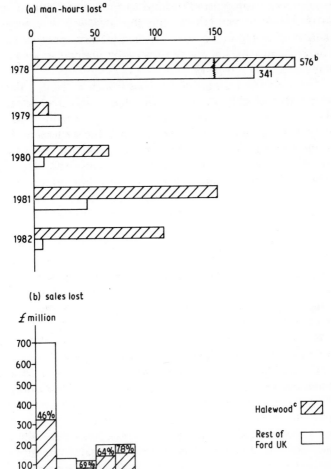

Figure 6 Sales and working time losses at Halewood

(a) man-hours lost[a]

(b) sales lost

Halewood[c]

Rest of
Ford UK

Source: Economist 26 March, 1982
Notes:
[a]Per 1000 hourly paid workers.
[b]Includes pay strike.
[c]Body and assembly only.

were difficult to reform and 1983 opened with a dispute prompted by supervisors' refusal to train direct operatives and an outbreak of vandalism, and the company was accused of using hard discipline to force through working practice changes. The efficiency package was resisted by manual unions both at plant and national level.

This was the background to the so-called 'Kelly' dispute in which an assembly worker of that name was dismissed for an alleged act of vandalism. The dispute lasted from 8 March to 7 April and, as with the Cowley dispute, the settlement involved an independent inquiry – this time under ACAS auspices – into the dismissal. Kelly was ultimately reinstated, the inquiry suggesting that the punishment did not fit the crime. However, the issues underlying the dispute were, once more, complex. During the strike, the company told the joint works committee that, within eight days of a return to work, they would be implementing changed working practices in the *body* plant, laid off without pay during the dispute. The body plant convenor found a close link between the two issues. He stated: 'They are trying to soften the men up for the real attack on work practices. They hope that when we come back we will be broke and have no stomach for another fight.'

Working practices had long been a problem. In 1980, the plant experienced a dispute over the introduction of new work rotas. In 1981 and 1982 further disputes over discipline, demarcation, and production standards gave Halewood shares of 14.6 per cent and 12.6 per cent of the industry's working days lost. The Kelly dispute led to a rise in conflict share to 39 per cent in 1983 (based on *Table 12*). After the Kelly dispute was resolved, efficiency-based changes began to be introduced, assisted by the establishment of a joint working party including national union officials, although these changes stopped short of breaking down established skill divisions.

Improvements in efficiency rather than technical change were the main causes of both these disputes. Nevertheless, in both cases the centralization of bargaining had made local grievances over pay, and consequent disputes, difficult to resolve. Where the companies attempted to change standards of discipline and effort without negotiation, an obvious response from employees was to strike. Moreover, such strikes were mostly of long

Table 12 *Working time*[a] *and vehicle losses in the three main manufacturers*

	BL		Ford		Vauxhall	
	days (ooos)	cars (ooos)	days (ooos)	cars (ooos)	days (ooos)	cars (ooos)
1974	–	–	484.6	79.4	–	–
1975	7,987.4	115.6	230.8	37.4	–	–
1976	–	–	185.4	39.7	12.5	5.0
1977	3,375.0	251.5	370.9	81.7	413.5	30.1
1978	1,312.5	131.3	2,726.0	168.8	52.3	18.5
1979	1,850.0	123.8	71.2	25.0	637.4	54.3
1980	437.5	51.7	56.4	26.5	13.8	8.5
1981	380.0	44.8	370.6	41.8	15.0	1.5
1982	275.0	9.7	157.0	35.5	21.7	2.0
1983	187.5	27.8	207.2	27.4	41.3	5.2

Source: Company figures.

Note: a. Working hour losses are standardized into eight-hour day losses.

duration because of the absence of a mutually acceptable machinery for compromise. The disputes have been over fair effort bargains rather than simply over pay, and over job property rights arising out of the increased mobility and flexibility now required of employees.

Thus much of the strike activity since 1980 can be explained in terms of the refusal of those workers employed in particular plants where new product launches provide a modicum of security to acquiesce in effort bargain changes and the surrender of job property rights. Although the institutional context of such disputes has changed radically from that accused by Turner, Clack, and Roberts (1967) of 'obsolescence' it remains incapable of accommodating such expectations primarily because, as we have shown, it is dominated by concerns with process efficiency and is founded on a rather rigid conception of management rights.

However, this picture of strike activity remains incomplete. So far, we have focused on stoppages above the size threshold recorded by the DE, and in the identification of stoppages by manufacturer we have relied on the DE list of principal stoppages, which requires the loss of 5,000 working days. As a consequence we have dealt with only a fraction of time lost through strike activity. Moreover, there is substantial under-reporting of that proportion of strike activity which does fall within the DE threshold definitions (Brown 1981; Edwards 1982). In the next section, we seek to remedy this by looking at manufacturers' in-house figures.

STRIKES BY MANUFACTURER

The major manufacturers each have their own system of recording time lost through disputes. Although these differ, it is possible to compare two series of figures – man hours lost and vehicles lost – across manufacturers, provided that the problems inherent in the analysis of these data are borne in mind.

First, management information systems differ between manufacturers so that differences in apparent strike proneness may simply be a function of differences in the rigour of reporting incidents, and changes within a company over time may follow from the improvement or dilapidation of procedures. Moreover, since the companies collect data on the basis of hours lost, the strike definition may embrace union meetings that overrun or simply delays in the resolution of grievances which all parties would not unequivocally define as strike action. In addition the figures are collected as part of the appraisal of plant performance from which political considerations are not isolated. On occasion, there may be the temptation to inflate or reduce the recorded level of conflict.

A further problem concerns working days lost through stoppages outside the company. In BL, since 1980, no such losses have been experienced although in earlier years supplier stoppages and involvement in the EEF-CSEU dispute in 1979 accounted for a substantial proportion of working days lost. Vauxhall, although relatively highly integrated, suffered losses through supplier strikes during this stoppage and again the following year during the steel strike. Only Ford appears to have been immune from external stoppages throughout the entire period.

However, the manufacturer's strike figures are important. They are the basis upon which the companies assess their own industrial relations performance. Moreover they are the only systematic evidence on the very *small* stoppages within the industry, which cumulatively may be as economically as important as larger ones.

The basic data on the three main manufacturers is presented in *Table 12*. The two most important observations are the absence of any simple proportional relationship between working days lost and lost production, and the effect of including small stoppages on the position of BL relative to Ford and Vauxhall.

The figures are dominated by the huge scale of losses recorded by BL. Even allowing for some differences in recording practice, the period 1977–79 was one in which BL's strike problem on their own measures was substantially worse than their competitors. This reverses the impression given by the official figures on major stoppages. Although BL avoided a large pay stoppage, its losses from smaller disputes during the parity programme produced a substantial competitive disadvantage. From the companies' own figures, it is also clear that the situation had been remedied by 1983. *Table 13* compares incidence and impact figures for three main manufacturers: a continuous series is only available for the period 1977–83.

The main pattern to emerge is the improvement in BL's strike record. The years 1979–80 were peaceful at Ford after the major pay dispute of 1978, but a higher level of conflict subsequently increased there. Columns 4–6 of *Table 13* show how many working days had to be lost to lose one vehicle's worth of production. Because the losses referred to are of production rather than sales, the figures conceal the differential economic impact of strikes on Ford, who can import similar models to make up the deficit, compared with BL who cannot.

It is perhaps best to look at the three series separately. In BL, strikes at Longbridge in 1980–81 and at Cowley in 1983 caused considerable vehicle losses which were high relative to man-day losses because strikes occurred on the highly productive new model lines. At Ford, the lowest impact per working day

Table 13 *Incidence and impact rates major car manufacturers 1977–83*

year	working days lost per 1,000 workers			working days lost per vehicle		
	Ford	BL	Vauxhall	Ford	BL	Vauxhall
1977	5,080	17,307	13,692	4.5	13.4	13.7
1978	36,837	6,836	1,570	16.2	10.0	2.8
1979	937	10,452	19,429	2.9	14.9	11.7
1980	770	2,787	475	2.1	8.5	1.6
1981	5,434	3,016	714	8.9	8.5	1.6
1982	2,368	2,546	1,033	4.4	28.4	10.85
1983	3,397	1,820	1,966	7.6	6.74	7.9

Source: Company figures on disputes. Employment from annual reports.

lost was during the 1978 pay dispute; there are probably at least three factors underlying this. The first is that, as a national dispute it involved direct and indirect workers. The second is that it occurred in September and October, after the August sales peak and because programme production volumes are related to seasonal patterns of demand a strike in October would be less damaging than one in July. Third, Ford had not recently launched new models whose production could be interrupted. Subsequently, in 1979–80, when market share was expanding rapidly, the impact of disputes was severe. Ford sought to raise output on the UK facilities in 1979 after the strike losses in 1978, while in 1980 two disputes at the Halewood plant prior to the Mark 3 Escort launch proved damaging.

There are certain parallels between the pattern at Vauxhall and Ford. At Vauxhall, too, longer strikes tend to be less damaging on the days-per-vehicle measure, while the low-conflict year of 1980 was one of high vulnerability. Since 1981, as employment has stabilized and market share and sales have improved, the company appears less vulnerable.

How, then, does this relate to Turner, Clack, and Roberts's view that strike losses may serve to shed labour surplus in the short term? The figures of *Table 13* argue for a more cautious approach. Strikes by direct workers on new model lines, either around the launch or in the run up to the August sales peak will be extremely damaging in terms of vehicles lost per days wages saved. Disputes by workers in plants where redundancies are planned because of product market difficulties may fit the Turner mould. In BL, this is effectively the contrast between the early finishing dispute and the 1982 dispute in Leyland vehicles. At Ford, where the possibility of import substitution changes the basis of all such calculations, there is the less extreme contrast between the 1978 autumn pay dispute and the relatively much more problematic disputes at Halewood in 1980.

Within plants, vulnerability to strikes varies over time. Despite the fluctuations introduced since 1980 by new model launches at different times of the year, all major manufacturers tend to produce more in the first six months of the year.[4] The third quarter is disrupted by holidays, while the fourth is the period where annual pay reviews take place, and it is perhaps here that, other things being equal, employers' anxiety over stoppages are least. Of course, the corollary for employees, who actually *take* strike action, is that concessions by the employers may be more forthcoming in May and June or just after new model launch. The events at Cowley and Halewood in 1983 bear witness to this, although in both cases the strikes were responses to easily identified managerial actions.

In general, however, recent events have been characterized rather by a concern to shed labour in the long term while launching new models than by the search for a cyclical adjustment mechanism. The four major companies have all shed labour overall since 1979 (in BL's case since 1977), but principally through voluntary redundancy which implies more or less permanent severance. While some disputes during the period may have been short-term adjustments to seasonal product market contraction or to other difficulties there is little evidence of collusive or employer-engineered disputes.

Data on the causes of such stoppages are available in detail for one of the four major car plants for two separate periods – for the third quarter of 1982 (July to September) and the first of 1984 (January to March) (*Table 14*). These were respectively the quarters of lowest and highest production. Data from one plant can only be illustrative.

Table 14 *Stoppages in a car plant by cause*

cause	period 1 (3rd quarter 1982)		period 2 (1st quarter 1984)	
	stoppages	total time lost	stoppages	total time lost
	no.	%	no.	%
work assignment/ labour mobility	9	34.2	11	91.5
pay	4	58.9	4	0.3
line speeds/ time allowances	5	2.5	4	0.2
discipline	2	1.7	3	0.2
TU facilities/ availability of steward	—	—	—	2.0
other	4	2.6	3	5.8
total	24	100.0	25	100.0
total working time lost (hours)	—	1,306.0	—	21,263.0
mean duration of stoppages (hours)	—	1.6	—	3.6
mean no. of workers involved	29.7	—	44.6	
vehicles lost	387.0	—	3,424.0	—
mean hours lost per vehicle	—	3.4	—	6.2

Source: Company records.

First, the pattern of industry differs from that noted more generally by Turner, Clack, and Roberts (1967). They remark that strikes tend to be fewer when demand is low, but that their size and duration tend to increase substantially so that the overall total of working days lost is higher (p. 332). In this plant, the number of strikes and their average duration were both greater: overall, sixteen times as many working days were lost, and nearly nine times as many vehicles.

The second rather surprising feature is that the plant was

more vulnerable to vehicle loss in the slack period. There was a substantial difference in product demand between the two periods. On top of the seasonal effect, the plant had launched a new model between the two periods and period 2 was the run-up quarter to the launch of a second. The explanation reveals the complexity of the questions concerning the impact of strikes on production. In period 1, 96 per cent of vehicles recorded as 'lost' in the quarter occurred in three disputes over a period of three shifts in one direct area: these disputes accounted for only 58 per cent of working time lost. A short dispute over line speeds led to two much larger ones over payment for time lost. In effect, then, 42 per cent of time lost did not lead to vehicle losses. In the second period 76 per cent of vehicles lost occurred in a large stoppage over redeployment which accounted for 91 per cent of working time lost. The remaining 9 per cent of working time lost, mainly in very short stoppages, was thus relatively costly, with a hours lost/vehicles lost ratio of 2:3.

This, of course, is a rather more expected pattern, time lost being more costly in a period of high demand. But the two quarters illustrate the importance of considerations of strike size (in terms both of duration and workers involved), timing (whether at the start or end of a shift), sequence (series of strikes in one area may run down buffer stocks and thus raise vehicle losses), and location (whether on direct or indirect work). Some strikes, such as support for the TUC day of action in period 2, were more fully anticipated and therefore had relatively a small impact.

The full distribution of stoppages by cause is given in *Table 14*. Across the two periods the main sources of conflict were work assignments and labour mobility. In period 2, this accounted for practically all strike activity if one excludes support for the TUC day of action (classified here as 'other'). Pay stoppages accounted for more time lost in the lower output period. This plant operated an output-related bonus scheme, and, when bonuses were lower than expected, 'downers' often occurred in protest, and disputes over lay-off pay were more likely. Line-speed disputes accounted for about the same absolute amount of time lost in both periods.

However, in period 2 a relatively large number of disputes

(but a small percentage of working time lost) occurred because of the unavailability of stewards, and there was some conflict at the same time in the plant about recent further reductions in shop steward facilities.

In short, small stoppages focus around job property rights, and specifically around the extent of mobility required. This contrasts with the forms of large-scale conflict around work-pace and bell-to-bell working. The explanation of the difference between the two periods is as follows. During periods of lower output there is concern with pay levels which also induces a concern with line speeds and the 'effort' side of the employment contract. During periods of higher output, pay levels rise but the degree of mobility and flexibility required generates conflict: this may also cause unavailability of stewards. Since conflict levels are much higher in period 2 there does not appear to be support for the 'labour surplus' view of conflict.

Ideally, one would like comparable data from other plants. However, it does receive some support from *Table 12* above detailing large stoppages.

In 1981 and 1983 large non-pay disputes occurred during the first two quarters of the year, or, as in BL in November 1981, where work standards were being tightened on new model lines. The occurrence of pay disputes between July and November is, of course, a function of bargaining dates as much as of pay discontent being higher at those times. However, if pay discontent in bonus plants is usually higher in low output periods, this raises questions about the scheduling of pay bargaining during the autumn.

CONCLUSION

Between 1974 and 1983 the characteristics of strike activity in the car industry underwent a fundamental change. Many of the features which Turner, Clack, and Roberts identified as factors underlying the assumed pattern of conflict in the 1960s disappeared. After 1974, the nature of the product market changed. After 1979, the labour market began steadily to contract. Moreover, by 1980 those institutional features which had occupied an important place in their explanation of observed patterns had disappeared.

The period contained two rather distinct phases of conflict. The first, roughly from 1977 to 1979, focused on pay. Strike losses at BL during the parity programme were huge, while the other major manufacturers all experienced large-scale pay stoppages in the later phases of the social contract. Both the long-term relative decline of car workers' earnings and the relative immunity of wage levels at BL were important factors in the generation of unfavourable 'fair wage' comparisons at this stage. In the second phase, 1980–83, the focus is on non-pay issues. Typically, conflict occurs over effort levels and job rights in high-output, retooled plants: these plants account for a far greater share of conflict than of employment. In both Ford and BL, similar management styles and similar collective bargaining arrangements tend to promote similar patterns of conflict.

The most important surviving features of Turner, Clack, and Roberts's explanation are thus the sets of worker expectations they identify. In their resistance to more tightly drawn effort standards and the reduction of rest allowances, employees may be seen to state a conception of fair wages for fair effort. In their resistance to more rigid disciplinary rules and enhanced mobility they are expressing a view on job rights. Despite, therefore, the reverses suffered by trade union organization, particularly in BL, and the frequently voiced opinion that car firm employees are now more realistic about the levels of effort required for competitiveness, there remains a degree of commitment to norms of effort and of employment rights which both management concerned with production continuity and trade unions concerned with the maintenance of employment must take into account.

SEVEN
TRADE UNION
STRATEGY IN
THE MOTOR
INDUSTRY

In this chapter we explore the response of the car workers and their unions to the various changes described in this book. Principally these include the technical innovations in the production process, the plant closures and shedding of labour, and the reorganization of working practices in each firm. In the broader context the response has to be seen in terms of the problem of competitiveness confronting British motor manufacturers at the beginning of the last decade. Because labour performance was seen as an important part of this problem, a common objective of the firms was to attempt to weaken or constrain the union organizations within the plants, although, as we shall see, the details of each firm's labour strategy did vary. In general, however, it is the changing product market and the internationalization of production which provides the context of these new strategies for labour and explains why the formerly powerful organizations of the car workers proved so vulnerable. Yet it is argued that the structure of union organization also impeded their response. Developed in the boom conditions of the post-war expansion, the plant-based and sectionalized union structure was too decentralized to provide a cohesive defence of their members' interests in the crises of the late 1970s. So, within the general theme of the weakening of labour's position the chapter analyses the reversals it experienced and the efforts to develop new means of coming to terms with the changed climate of car production.

THE DEVELOPMENT OF SHOP-FLOOR ORGANIZATION

In the post-war boom of the car industry the trade unions made considerable advances in organization and by the mid-1960s the car workers appeared indomitable. They had achieved relatively high wage levels and had a reputation for militant action, particularly over their extensive job controls. Industrial relations in the car industry provoked government alarm and persistent media attention. Yet during the crisis of the late 1970s, as imports were sucked into the British market and demand contracted under the second major oil price rise in the decade, the unions appeared unable to resist the determination of the car firms to raise productivity, improve process efficiency by revising working standards unilaterally, impose stricter discipline and a stronger policy against unofficial disputes, and even make wholesale plant closures.

How then could the pendulum swing so rapidly away from labour? To understand, we have to look at the basis of union organization in the plants and the conditions under which it flourished before examining the strategies by which the car firms sought to constrain or weaken it.

The British motor industry has traditionally been character-ized by strong shop-floor organizations based around individual plants and with a number of unions competing in overlapping job territories for membership. This decentralized union structure emerged through the way in which production was organized because, traditionally, the British-owned firms centred around the Midlands opted to work on piece-rate systems. Through these they could secure high output with relatively little supervision and the delegation of production problems such as parts shortages or machine breakdowns to the operatives themselves.

Yet once the trade unions were recognized for the semi-skilled areas, piece-work negotiation presented an opportunity to extend membership and to gain considerable controls over the way work was organized. This came about because most firms were selling into a home market protected by tariffs and into expanding export markets and so were primarily concerned to meet the strong demand for their products with little regard for cost rises. They were prepared, informally at least, to concede to shop-floor representatives a bargaining function over piece-rate prices in return for high output.

Negotiations on the shop floor were, to use the terminology of the Donovan Report a decade later, 'informal'. Agreements were unwritten and stewards were reliant upon 'custom and practice' as the basis of their claims, in contrast to the contractual precision of local agreements in the American industry for instance (Katz 1984). The process of unionization was not uniform though. Partly because of employer hostility it was slower in BMC's larger assembly plants at Longbridge and Cowley for instance and Tolliday and Zeitlin (1982) estimate that only 25 per cent of the work-force in Morris Motors was unionized in 1956. Lapsed members were also a problem, especially with the repeated lay-offs in the industry. Complete unionization of the production areas was not achieved until the 1960s and it was in the smaller British firms that shop-floor organization was strongest, at the Standard, Rootes, and Daimler companies – although these firms did appear to have a general effect on wages throughout the industry (Turner, Clack, and Roberts 1967: ch. 5).

In the American firms shop-floor organization also remained more retarded. At Ford, continued insistence upon management prerogative over the organization and pace of work meant that the stewards had relatively little influence and all pay negotiations were conducted with national officials. Subsequently, industrial relations at Dagenham were marked by sharp conflicts over control of the shop floor in which the rights of stewards became a central area of dispute. The climaxes of this struggle were two disputes over the sacking of shop stewards, one in 1957 being the 'bell-ringer' dispute,[1] and the other in 1962 when seventeen stewards were dismissed. In each case courts of inquiry were held to resolve the case;[2] in each case the stewards remained dismissed, and as a result shop-floor organization remained weak until the mid-1960s.

In contrast the other American-owned company, Vauxhall, experienced considerably less conflict with the shop floor. Initially recognizing only two unions (the AEU and the NUVB) in 1942, Vauxhall pursued a more accommodating policy whilst adopting a day-rate pay system similar to Ford in 1956 which was negotiated with national officials. A joint management committee operated as a sort of works council and consultation was more institutionalized than in the other firms. Perhaps Vauxhall's peaceful labour relations were also related to the flexibility built into the wage structure which allowed for grade progression and developed job ladders for the semi-skilled grades, and to Luton's isolation from the main centres of production (Goldthorpe *et al.* 1968). Vauxhall experienced major disputes in the 1960s and again more recently, but the shop-floor organization at Luton has never been as well organized or aggressive as at Ellesmere Port or elsewhere in the industry.

It can be seen, then, that there was a general drive by car workers to establish controls over their particular work loads and this was associated with the growth of union membership. Having established a degree of control it was then possible to regulate the pace and effort required of a job as well as exerting some leverage to resist undesirable changes, or at least to extract a price for them. As a strategy the attempt to limit managerial prerogative was directed towards increasing job security and regularity of earnings in response to the cyclical nature of the product market. What clouds the notion of a coherence behind the actions of the shop stewards was the decentralized level at which bargaining took place, the piecemeal and uneven progress in establishing controls, and the characteristically informal nature of the process, for the official unions had very little influence upon day-to-day activities and rarely developed or transmitted specific bargaining objectives to the shop floor. Indeed, writing at the height of shop-floor power Turner, Clack, and Roberts (1967) characterized the situation as one of 'parallel unionism' with the shop-steward organizations being the 'real union' and the formal national bodies largely irrelevant to everyday affairs (pp. 216–23). The loyalties of car workers would therefore be strongly orientated towards their own work groups or, most broadly, bound by a factory consciousness (Beynon 1984).

From the late 1960s this aggressive decentralization was more openly encouraged by the national officials of the major general unions. Under the leadership of Jack Jones, the TGWU shifted to supporting a more central role in negotiations for stewards. It also created closer links between them and the official branch structures, a policy which was in part based on Jones's experience at Standard Motors just after the war where plant bargaining was pioneered (Melman 1958). In the AEU, Hugh Scanlon also encouraged a devolution of power to the shop stewards, reflecting a philosophy that the wishes of the rank and file should determine the policies and actions of the leadership, in contrast to the more autocratic style of leadership of the union 'bosses' of the 1950s.

Although many of the difficulties created by multi-unionism were offset by the elaborate shop-steward organizations, coherence could be still undermined by inter-union and sectional rivalries (Batstone, Boraston, and Frenkel 1977). The establishment of the closed shop in each of the major firms in the early 1970s also stabilized recruiting lines, reducing inter-union disputes, but with the reassertion of management control in the late 1970s and the introduction of new technology, divisions between unions once again became of some importance. Yet at its height the power of shop-floor organizations in the car industry was sufficient to create deep concern in official circles mainly due to the continuing spiral of earnings and work stoppages in the 1960s (Durcan, McCarthy, and Redman 1983). Official inquiries were concerned over several major disputes in various companies including Austin, Ford, Morris, and Rover and a common theme in each was the role and powers of shop stewards in the plants.[1] Under Sir Jack Scamp, a Motor Industry Joint Labour Council was also convened to try to develop procedural reforms which would reduce the amount of disputes then occurring and much of the Donovan Commission (1968) was based upon the engineering industry's problems in general and the car industry in particular, which at the time directly and indirectly employed over 1 million people.

This shop-floor power was based upon the long and large

expansion of the demand for cars after the war, which was almost completely met from domestic manufacturers. With high employment, bargaining at the point of production enabled car workers to exploit their power to the full in negotiating over the frequent production changes occasioned by technical innovation or product revisions. For their part, with a priority of achieving high output to meet market demand, managers were inclined to accede and pass on the extra costs.

Yet even in its heyday there were clear limits to shop-floor power. First, the picture varied considerably between plants. Whilst the degree of control exerted by semi-skilled workers in the car firms over their jobs was comparatively high, it remained limited to production tasks. Other areas of management authority such as finance, model design, and development were uncontested. Second, although the pursuit of job controls by less skilled groups did limit managerial prerogative they were never so formally established as the unilateral controls of the crafts which were reinforced by limiting labour supply. Leverage by reference to custom and practice, upon which the less-skilled groups relied, occurred through the opportunities presented by managerial mistakes ('errors of omission') as well as by the exigencies of production (Brown 1973). Gains were thus often unevenly spread, and under piece-work the iniquities in pay between different work groups were pronounced. The degree of job control established by different work groups was also uneven, being partly dependent upon the vigilance of the steward for maintenance and the ability to generalize such changes as did occur was strongly dependent upon the 'leadership' qualities of the stewards' organization (Batstone, Boraston, and Frenkel 1977). Work groups were thus competing against each other to maintain their pay positions as well as against managerial control, so that their aspirations were sectional and fragmented. Moreover, the strategy of job control could not secure continuous employment. As was noted in the last chapter, the rising number of strikes in the industry during the 1960s were associated with lay-offs and interruptions to work, which on occasion the firms could use to their advantage to adjust to changing product market conditions. Many of these shortcomings were subsequently exploited by managements as they tried to come to terms with the power of the shop floor.

Industry crises in the 1970s

Despite being built on the expansion of the industry in the post-war boom, the strength of the plant-based organizations was largely unshaken by the first major shock of the oil price rise of 1973. In fact the crisis that ensued in the industry appeared to be resolved relatively favourably for the car workers. First, although output never fully recovered from the 1972 peak the rescues of BLMC and Chrysler which followed both brought in government funding and renewed expansion proposals. The other American firms also remained committed to British manufacture despite a faltering performance from Vauxhall.

Second, in BLMC and Chrysler formal participation schemes were introduced giving the stewards an input into new areas of decision-making. So although Lord Ryder's recovery plan for BLMC did not adopt the trade unions' proposals that worker directors should be elected, his participation scheme was endowed by the CSEU and a majority of shop-floor representatives. Previously a proposal for consultation made in 1970 by management had been rejected on the shop floor as potentially undermining its bargaining power. Now, public ownership seemed to offer a new form of industrial partnership in which past criticisms of under-investment and insecurity would be remedied by substantial funding for new models and expanded output. Similar optimism surrounded the Chrysler deal in 1975 although the firm remained in private hands.

Third, attempts by BLMC and Chrysler to reform the work-place bargaining arrangements and extend managerial control were only partially implemented. The shop-floor organizations were able to retain a degree of bargaining power. From around 1970 both firms tried to imitate Ford's labour strategy by moving away from piece-work to day-rates, but resistance on the shop floor and fear of prolonged stoppages meant that these firms were unable or unwilling to establish fully centralized control over pay. Wage negotiations remained sufficiently decentralized for persistent leap-frogging pressure to be maintained even if the rates of increase in wages did slow. Day-rate plants began to see wages drop below those which continued with piece-rates; but this was compensated by a new focus on the effort side of the bargain, for the principle of 'mutuality', required the steward's agreement for any proposed change to work methods. Management inexperience in organizing production under the new system compounded the problems. The net result was that productivity in BLMC and Chrysler fell dramatically. Both firms then began to feel the effects of foreign competition from the Japanese and other European producers after Britain's tariff barriers were removed with entry to the EEC. Yet during this period in the mid-1970s, the union organizations at national level and on the shop floor assumed a stronger level of government support would guarantee that expansion could continue, so little thought was given to alternative bargaining strategies. It was thus assumed through-out the industry that the shop stewards would continue to provide the most effective means of representation for their members; in Ford, for example, the lay officials were looking forward to wresting exclusive control of the NJNC from the full-time officials (Passingham and Connor 1977). In Chrysler and British Leyland it was thought that the steward hierarchies could adjust to new demands upon them in co-operating with management in the participation schemes. Fears of 'incorporation' were overruled.[2]

With hindsight, then, the trade unions were lulled into a false sense of security. Failure to push through earlier bargaining reforms, the optimistic expansion plans, and new participation exercises suggested a secure future. They were therefore taken by surprise when strengthening competition led to falling demand for British cars and the deep commercial crises of the late 1970s. The long expansionary boom on which the shop-floor organizations had grown rapidly came to an end. Although government support was not withdrawn it became more qualified by political sensitivity to the funding of losses and the continuing high level of disputes, particularly those over pay, which represented a direct challenge to the incomes policy then in force. Because several national officials were closely identified with the government's policies and with the NEB's plan for British Leyland (Harry Urwin, Deputy General

Secretary of the TGWU was influential in setting up the Leyland participation scheme through his position on the NEB, for example) divisions within the union movement began to emerge and it was in this context that managements of the three weaker firms – BL, Talbot, and Vauxhall – began to confront the power of the shop floor. But even in Ford, which was relatively successful in the market-place (and latterly Vauxhall as well), the trade unions have been subdued to some extent, as we saw in the first section of the chapter. Quite how each took on the trade unions is considered next.

MANAGERIAL STRATEGIES

To an extent each firm adopted its own range of strategies depending on the position it was in at the end of the 1970s, but with the common objective of sustaining competitive production in an increasingly competitive market. Each sought therefore to break down the principal source of resistance to managerial authority, the shop-floor organization based around the stewards, by mixing policies of accommodation and direct confrontation. These were in a sense not new. The novelty of the period was the sophisticated methods of communication developed to bypass the stewards and drive home the picture of intensive competition in the market-place and its implications for labour. Through this strategy the ordinary workers – the rank-and-file members – became distinguishable as a separate group whose interests did not always coincide with that of their representatives and in exploiting these differences the key sanction deployed by the foreign firms was the threat of diverting production abroad. How far the trade unions have been able to come to terms with this and the way they propose to do so in the future constitutes much of the discussion in the rest of the chapter. The home-based manufacturer, BL, was never able to use the same sort of lever though and as a publicly owned company was protected to some extent from the impact of the market. It therefore had to adopt a unique set of strategies and we start by examining how its managers pushed through the dramatic reforms of the last few years.

BL

Fundamental changes to the roles and relationship between managers, lay and national union officials, and the rank and file were implemented at BL under Michael Edwardes. In particular the position of the stewards as intermediaries between managers and employees was challenged through the strategy of 'direct communications'. To initiate such a strategy, however, Edwardes first had to obtain agreement from the government through the NEB that his board's authority would not be overruled. This he obtained partly because of BL's increasing losses and partly because the company's continuing strike record was a political embarrassment to the Labour government (Edwardes 1983).

Edwardes declared the reassertion of management control on the shop floor as crucial to the very survival of the business. From 1978 onwards and in response initially to a series of disputes over working practices and internal pay relativities his strategy of 'direct communications' was developed in several ways. This was designed to inform employees directly and individually of the management's intentions to re-establish BL's commercial viability in the shortest possible time. It was also made clear that management would be prepared to close parts of the business if necessary rather than capitulate to opposition to its plans from the work-force. Letters were sent during disputes reiterating the firm line. To seize the initiative managers also called for ballots of the whole work-force to gain acceptance in principle to important changes such as the Recovery Plan, formulated in 1979, which signalled the formal demise of the Ryder expansion plan. In addition, senior managers began to counter what they saw as media bias which meant that only the shop stewards were putting their case to the public. In radio and television broadcasts the 'company's' case was developed as well as through newspaper advertisements. Subsequently, the strategy was refined by such methods as sending letters out at the start of pay negotiations rather than waiting for the breakdown in talks. In the 1984 dispute letters were addressed to employees' wives to ensure, as Edwardes had previously put it, that employees could calmly and deliberately consider the situation with their families' (1983: 93).

These sorts of tactics have usually been associated with a strong reluctance by management to make significant concessions beyond its opening offer in pay negotiations. Challenging the steward organization also involved managers insisting on addressing mass meetings or calling their own to put their case. The central thrust of the strategy was therefore to suggest that given the commercial position of the business, shop steward opposition was not in the best interests of the ordinary employees.

BL's strategy was not to dispense with trade unions but instead to reduce the control of the shop stewards over their members: 'On the contrary, it was to rebalance the whole order of things so that together with management national officials would be able to play a proper role without finding their authority eroded by strong stewards, weak management, and a lack of understanding of what management was trying to achieve' (Edwardes 1983: 79–80).

Thus the centralization of pay bargaining actually brought national officials to the forefront once more, simultaneously reducing the influence of the stewards and local full-time officials. Dealing with the national officers meant that BL's management could put pressure on them to oppose unofficial disputes and to isolate any resistance on the shop floor by not making stoppages official. Where the national officials wavered, the threat of closure rather than concession was restated, and because this would have meant a substantial loss of jobs and members throughout the engineering industry, it was something they had to take very seriously. The union leaders therefore found themselves obliged to support some of BL's hardest decisions, such as the Recovery Plan, which involved the loss of 25,000 jobs, despite opposing redundancy in principle. Specifically, this followed from the commitment obtained by Edwardes from the CSEU at the beginning of his chairmanship to the basic proposition that a return to competitive production was the only long-term guarantee of survival. From this BL's management was able to argue that any opposition voiced by the unions to their recovery proposals was inconsistent and that they had to accept some surgery (in the form of closures) to preserve the business as a whole. Indeed one senior manager did use the analogy of severing a limb to keep the body alive in describing the rationale behind reducing the size of the business. The national officials therefore found themselves in the apparently contradictory position of endorsing management actions against the interests of certain sections of their membership as well as against the trade union organization in the plants. Recently this strategy was further extended when, in the view of the company, the national unions failed to discipline the shop-floor leaders; the company then took punitive action against them. In November, 1984, it invoked the new Trade Union Act to attack the strike balloting methods used prior to a pay dispute and called for individual secret postal voting.

This is not to say that there was subsequently no union opposition. Yet where it did develop it was undermined by the exploitation of institutional divisions within the CSEU. In particular this allowed the isolation of the TGWU, which was most strongly opposed to the contraction plan and should, as the union with the largest membership, have been the dominant voice. On occasion disunity was even fostered by astute use of the press, as during the 1981 pay negotiations when Edwardes himself reported an apparent change of position by Alex Kitson, the TGWU's negotiating leader, which threatened to provoke an official dispute against the wishes of the other representatives.

The differences between the national union officials, the rank and file, and the steward organizations emerged most crucially in the autumn of 1979 when the Recovery Plan was announced and Derek Robinson was dismissed. Robinson, as Longbridge convenor and chairman of the BL Combine Committee of stewards was in effect the leading lay representative in BL. He was dismissed for leading the shop-floor opposition to the Edwardes strategy and specifically for his authorship, with three other senior stewards, of a pamphlet called 'The Alternative Strategy to Edwardes'. His sacking provoked a walk-out at Longbridge that the TGWU supported by declaring official but this annoyed the AUEW executive who felt that as Robinson was a member of their union this was primarily their dispute. When subsequently warned by the BL board that an official dispute would not gain Robinson's reinstatement at any cost and that they would close Longbridge, the largest plant in the company, in the event of this taking place, the AUEW backed down. The dispute then subsided although it must be said that considerable numbers of the work-force had already ignored the strike call by the Longbridge stewards or returned to work. Official backing for a strike was proposed by the AUEW several months later after the union had held an internal inquiry, which found Robinson unfairly dismissed. By that time though the impetus had collapsed; Robinson stayed sacked and his colleagues disciplined.

Hyman (1983) has argued that Robinson's case was lost by the equivocation of his union. The unions were divided in the important period immediately following the dismissal and it is true that the political differences between Robinson, a Communist Party member, and the right-wing-dominated national executive meant that there was considerable antagonism between them. However, as an explanation of why the dismissal was successful it ignores the constraints upon the AUEW executive and the considerable uncertainty among the work-force about the consequences of taking action on Robinson's behalf. Just before the dispute BL's board had set out the deteriorating sales position of the company and its proposed remedies in the Recovery Plan. As this had been circulated to the whole work-force it was widely known that a long strike would be likely to result in the closure of the factory. Furthermore, the management successfully used a referendum to obtain the work-force's endorsement of the Plan in which 87 per cent voted in support. This result isolated Robinson, exposing him to the charge that he was not properly representing the views of his members but pursuing the fight against the Plan for political purposes. More directly, the fear of imminent job loss in the event of a dispute also contributed to the collapse of resistance. So the episode starkly demonstrated the central dilemma facing the car workers at this time in each of the firms: whether to resist change and increase the risk of the firm going out of business, or to accept unpopular decisions in the belief that they probably enhanced job security. It also revealed the extent to which the strategy of BL to divide the interests of the rank and file, the lay activists, and national officials was successful.

Robinson's sacking was a turning point in BL's industrial relations. It dissolved active opposition to the Recovery Plan which signalled the massive contraction of BL. It also demonstrated to the stewards management's determination to neutralize their influence. In the wake of this BL pushed through the reform of working practices in April, 1980, ending the mutuality agreements. No longer could job times be negotiated; the stewards' long-standing controls over the levels of effort required on the shop floor were thus ended and in some plants all discussions between stewards and managers were virtually terminated.

In this context and with the same sort of dilemmas confronting the various groups involved, BL was able to push through its closure programme, which started with the decision to close the Speke Number Two plant, where the TR7 sports car was built. Taken at the height of a prolonged strike over mutuality and manning levels at the plant, it highlighted the ambiguous position facing the national unions. For their close allegiance to the Labour government made then sensitive to the political unpopularity of a strike that appeared to be undermining Leyland's recovery, and the Speke dispute was never formally made official by the major union involved, the TGWU. Initially, the CSEU did oppose the closure decision; but the prospect of a 'major confrontation' which might jeopardize further investment and prompt wider redundancies led the confederation to revise its position and then to advise acceptance of closure (CSEU minutes, March–May, 1978).

Locally, inexperience in dealing with wholesale closure was shown in the inability to generate mass opposition either among the work-force or the community. While the timing of the closure decision at the end of a seventeen-week strike militated against a prolonged campaign there were only a couple a mass meetings called by the stewards to call for opposition. Wider union support was inhibited by the differences in the local structures of each union and the lukewarm response of the national officials in the Confederation. It also proved impossible to develop an effective political campaign; by 1978 the Labour government had accepted the need for closure to stem BL's losses, despite the local employment consequences, and even locally the stewards complained of indifference to their campaign from some MPs so that a broader-based community response never developed.[3]

With a problem of serious over-capacity it was also clear to workers in other plants that their prospects would be enhanced by Speke's closure. Competition for a reduced amount of resources heightened divisions: in particular the Canley workforce was unwilling to support wholly any campaign for Speke as it was to Canley that TR7 assembly was to be transferred. Such divisions undermined the chance of a broad shop-floor-based opposition to the contraction developing through the BL Combine Committee. Resistance was also undercut by the wide acceptance of an improved redundancy offer from the company, made on condition that the closure timetable and removal of plant and equipment were uninterrupted. It was a tactic that was used again by BL in its subsequent closures and by Peugeot when closing Linwood in Scotland in 1981.

In fact, each of the car firms has shed its labour without confrontation by offering voluntary redundancy rather than compulsory separations. And attempts to establish a rank-and-file opposition to job loss have easily been broken by this tactic. Plant occupations, seen earlier in the decade in shipbuilding, also appeared of little use: only in the Leyland trucks plant at Bathgate, Scotland, was this attempted in 1982, but as a tactic it offered little leverage in the depressed market conditions. At Speke, for example, the work-force were well aware of the stockpiling of TR7s which it had produced. Historically, the motor industry has had a tradition of relatively casual employment with frequent lay-offs even in the boom periods; perhaps the ready acceptance of redundancy was in some ways a legacy of this experience. Undoubtedly it has been a crucial factor in allowing the car firms to make their adjustments to the changed environment of the last decade.

THE FOREIGN-OWNED FIRMS; FORD, TALBOT, VAUXHALL

While BL's strategies reflected its deep commercial crisis, the other major manufacturer, Ford, remained more profitable and productive, and without the need to reassert management control so sharply. Nevertheless, Ford faced a well-organized work-force, aware of the company's exceptional prosperity, and keen to obtain a share of this through campaigns such as pay parity with the Midlands plants. Ford deployed a sophisticated mixture of strategies with some success. As Sander Meredeen, himself a one-time Ford manager, put it, the company realized in the late 1960s that it had to come to terms with the 'challenge from below'.

> 'This would only be achieved by replacing the traditional arm's length relationship between the company and its rank-and-file leaders with a clear, positive and business-like relationship. The Company's aim must be to produce Industrial Relations policies to a purposeful pattern ahead of the bargaining pressures. It must capture and retain the initiative rather than react to each crisis as it arose.'
>
> (Friedman and Meredeen 1980: 36).

The first fruit of this accommodating policy was the admission of five convenors to the NJNC in 1969. In the 1970s this line was extended; convenors were given more facilities and better contacts with Ford's central staff. They were drawn away from day-to-day issues as Ford tried to minimize pressure to bargain at the point of production. Procedural reforms such as the 1975 Works Standards Agreement were also designed to reduce shop-floor disputes. This shortened the dispute procedure so that work assignment grievances were resolved more rapidly, thereby reducing the likelihood of 'wildcat' stoppages. A *status quo* clause was also conceded in return for no industrial action over proposed changes to 'well established working practices' – in effect the stewards gained some influence over job standards. By 1978 the lay representatives had obtained a majority on the trade union side of the NJNC with convenors from each plant and some craft representatives getting seats.

On the other hand, Ford also pursued tighter discipline to secure high and continuous production. In the 1970s the company took to laying-off workers without notice in the event of unconstitutional action to enforce the use of procedures. This maximized the costs to the work-force of any local stoppage and was also detrimental to plant-wide solidarity. The tough line had its costs for the company though, with several serious disturbances occurring before it backed down by agreeing to pay for a full shift once the work-force had clocked on. Again Ford tried to raise the penalties for unconstitutional action in 1980 by introducing a new code of discipline; again, however, modifications followed after a dispute at Halewood; which was apparently aggravated by the new procedures (Beynon 1984: 357–66). As we saw in Chapter 5, however, Ford has persisted with disciplinary policies (with mixed success) as well as adopting forms of 'direct communication' with the work-force to achieve 'attitudinal changes'. Basically the message has been that current profitability is no guarantee of future success given increasing competition and the ability of the company to switch sourcing to its foreign plants.

Indeed, whatever the successes of Ford's work-force in resisting tighter discipline and higher work-rates it has found its power deeply undermined by the corporate strategy of internationally integrated production. Thus from 1976, with the introduction of the Fiesta model, built in Spain and Germany as well as Dagenham, Ford's stewards were faced with a new dimension to multinational activity. For many years they had been aware of Detroit's influence on strategic planning. Now they were having to bargain for a share of European production, realizing that if British factories were no longer to supply the British market jobs could be lost despite Ford's market leadership.

On its own, internationally integrated sourcing was not necessarily detrimental to the interests of the British car workers. The volume of cars being produced was not thereby reduced and in theory it was possible for there to be more work if larger markets were to be supplied. It also reduced the dependence upon a single national market which could fluctuate in size. Hence Ford's Brigend plant supplies engines to a number of the company's European plants as well as the UK market, and British design technicians have a majority of the work of Ford Europe. The problem, however, has been that in practice, because of the comparatively low levels of efficiency in British operations in the past, the manufacturers have opted to discriminate against their UK plants in the allocation of work. Hence Ford chose to source the Granada and Capri models from abroad having previously made them in the UK. Component sourcing is also integrated internationally. GM brings engines from Australia and Brazil and power-train components from Japan for its European operations, including assembly in the Vauxhall plants. British assembly is therefore no longer an indicator of British manufacture (and this is the case with BL as well as the multinationals).

International sourcing therefore provides a powerful lever for the manufacturers that has had a profound influence on the bargaining strategies of the shop floor. No longer does a single plant build a single model for its own national market; companies can switch production between plants and supply components from a variety of sources. Duplicating production systems, as at Halewood and Saarlouis, enables efficiency comparisons to be made followed, as a general rule, by the imposition of the highest standards. At worst, the sanction for failing to achieve these could be the withdrawal of funds for future capital investment without which any plant becomes obsolete. And as plants compete for the next model generation so the productivity ratchet can be applied more tightly. In this way the plant-based trade union organization has been outflanked. No longer can a strong sales performance based on the output of a range of models each sourced from a single plant within a national market be the platform for aggressive shop-floor controls. Indeed such is the reversal of trade union power that while British workers at Ellesmere Port, at Ryton, and at Longbridge have had to relinquish their informal job controls and achieve European performance levels they have not been able to secure a restoration of former levels of relative pay. But how they have tried to respond to the internationalization of production as well as the other changes in the industry discussed in previous chapters forms the concluding section.

RESPONSES TO INTERNATIONAL PRODUCTION

The preceding discussion suggests that the unions have been unable to counter the threat effects on their bargaining power of international sourcing of car production. Nevertheless, a mixture of industrial and political strategies have been used with some success on specific issues and it is through the whole development of international production that unions became more interested in corporate strategy. This was a reactive move, however. It could only be a response to something that had already started because a campaign required the mobilization of rank-and-file opinion and this could only come from concrete events that were already under way. As one Ford convenor said:

'In Ford we saw a situation where jobs and models were being taken away from the United Kingdom. The classic case was the Granada. We no longer make the Granada in this country.... The worker sees in this the danger of finding himself out of a job.... They [the workers] ask themselves, is the company going to shift it all abroad and import the car? So they get interested and this stimulates the stewards.'
(Passingham and Connor 1977: 12–13)

In effect, though, this sort of response was only likely to heighten the problems facing the British car workers. Responding through the traditional methods of a shop-floor mobilization meant attempting to sustain the degree of control on production that had contributed to the relative inefficiency of the British industry, and prompted the decisions to switch to foreign sourcing. So although the campaigns were limited in their aims to preserving established patterns of production, the paradox was that they were only likely to provoke further out-sourcing. Furthermore the first major campaign, over the sourcing of Fiesta production in the mid-1970s, revealed the problems associated with any strategy based on collective bargaining as the company refused to discuss its sourcing policies on principle. The Dagenham stewards therefore adopted a political strategy, lobbying MPs and ministers, and broadened the issue by pointing out the implications for the British engineering and steel industries of foreign sourcing. In so far as discussions between Ford and politicans did take place and Fiesta production was established at Dagenham, the stewards felt the campaign was a success. But no longer-term guarantees were extracted from the company either about production at Dagenham or more broadly about its plans for British manufacture. Nor did this then become the basis for a more generalized political campaign to protect jobs in the motor industry by the national unions, and it was only at the end of the 1970s that the threat of international production was openly confronted. So the Fiesta campaign revealed but did not fully resolve the vulnerability of the British car workers to the corporate changes in the industry then taking place, organized as they were in plant-based union structures.

Subsequently as well, the election of a less sympathetic government has meant that political strategies are unlikely to be so influential. Thus the car workers have had to rely primarily on bargaining as their strategy, despite the reluctance of Ford (or any of the multinationals) to discuss sourcing plans. Indeed this has informally become the subject of constant negotiation within the plants. The sanctions applied include blacking of machinery such as dies to stop the export of production. At other times imports have been blocked; in 1981 the Dagenham body plant stopped panels coming in from Belgium until a different balance of output had been agreed, for instance. But in such campaigns the role of overt action is usually limited, with trade-offs including the willingness to accept new working practices (rather than merely agreeing to them formally) as well as pay and conditions claims, because it is recognized that to push the balance too far *could* result in the wholesale relocation of production in the longer run. The stewards have also had to develop some awareness of market trends throughout Europe enabling them to aim for the most favourable production combinations; thus past reductions in sales of the Escort model throughout Europe as buyers switched to the Fiesta and the relative failure of the Sierra to live up to the sales of its predecessor, the Cortina, have influenced their priorities. Experience has suggested that to be over-reliant upon a single model can prove to be a mistake, as was shown by Ford Germany's dependence upon the ageing Granada.

Another important lesson is that as blocking the import of vehicles or components has become an important sanction the car workers have become more dependent on outside groups. In this respect, the S-car dispute at Vauxhall, and less publicly the blocking of Fiesta imports during the 1978 dispute at Ford, demonstrated the advantages of general unionism, because in both cases it was the action of dock workers in agreeing to 'black' imports which was crucial.

In the S-car dispute at Vauxhall, protests arose over the proposal to import GM's Supermini (known as the Nova) from its then new Spanish plant at a time when there was only single shift working at Luton and Ellesmere Port, producing the Cavalier and Astra respectively. Vauxhall's UK market share was rising rapidly in this period but in 1981 it was still assembling a majority of its cars (55 per cent) abroad. Initially Vauxhall's management rejected requests for the Nova to be manufactured in the UK (its Zaragossa plant having sufficient capacity – 300,000 units per annum – to supply the whole of Europe) and for second shifts to be introduced at Ellesmere Port and Luton. Official backing for any dispute then came from each of the Vauxhall unions, and included a proposal to black any imports of the Nova when it was due to be introduced in March, 1983. Before this, however, GM proposed a new £38 million investment package: assembly of the forthcoming Cavalier estate from August, 1983 at Luton; the new Astra model to be assembled at Ellesmere Port from 1984; plus a new commercial vehicle to be built in the UK. Second shifts were also to be introduced at both car plants by August, 1984. Ostensibly the timing and outcome of this union action was highly successful, but precisely how much effect the union campaign had is difficult to assess. It is possible that GM were already considering further investment in the UK, although in the short term their plants in Belgium and Germany suffered short-time working while UK production rose.

This dispute demonstrated that in webs of international production sourcing, the ports and their workers have become the linchpins. The role of the TGWU in this dispute in securing agreement from its docker members was crucial, and to that extent it is a more advantageous form than industrial unionism. Co-operation and solidarity are not inevitable however. Otherwise, as one TGWU national official said, given their strategic position the dockers would be fighting someone else's battle every day, and in this instance the agreement to 'black' imports was conditional upon Vauxhall workers themselves 'showing their mettle'. Accordingly Vauxhall workers agreed at mass meetings to become involved in picketing at docks and any other necessary action in support of the dispute.

At other times inter-union rivalries appear to have undermined the trade unions' position. At Ellesmere Port, for instance, the TGWU dominated the assembly areas whilst the AUEW were predominant in the mechanical areas and maintenance. Differences in earnings between these sections due mainly to different levels of plant utilization tended to create sectional rivalries between the unions, with the AUEW areas resisting transfers from the assembly plant for fear of a reduction in overtime and shift premia. Subsequently the ending of power-train production in Vauxhall in 1980 had a disproportionately large effect upon the AUEW, but the response to this move, in which 2,000 jobs were lost, was influenced by divisions between the unions over the question of a campaign, over the bargaining on redundancy terms, and the relocation of AUEW members to TGWU sections. Similarly, at Dagenham efforts to develop a campaign against the foundry closure were also impeded by rivalry between the two semi-skilled unions over the negotiation of redundancy terms and transfers to other plants.

But within certain parameters the trade unions do appear to have had some influence on international sourcing decisions. Much of their strength lies outside their own organizational abilities and in the way the market works. Unionists as well as managers are aware of the importance of the British-built image for sales to fleet buyers. Moreover, as Britain remains a highly profitable market with lower wage levels than in Germany and Belgium, it makes sense for the foreign companies to get their British facilities operating efficiently rather than supply from abroad. Recognition of these advantages means that car workers face the threat not so much of total shutdown as the retention of the minimum facilities for a British-built image. As we have seen, Vauxhall exemplified this danger: its work-force dropped by over 30 per cent as its market share doubled between 1980 and 1984. In the same period a majority of the successful Cavalier models sold in the UK were built abroad, and according to Jones (1985) Vauxhall's average domestic content of its vehicles is so low as to raise doubts about its status as a British producer.

International trade unionism

Responding to the internationalization of production through links with unions abroad has also presented problems. On one level there are practical difficulties of resources and language barriers. Particularly at the shop-floor level the Ford stewards contrasted the efficient integration of management structures within the Ford Europe organization – where English is the standard business language – and the haphazard links with German and Spanish unions, without the benefits of telex machines and computer linkages. Thus comparative data on the relative efficiency of plants, overwhelmingly derived from management sources, cannot easily be checked by reference to union-originated data. Information flows also remain haphazard; as one steward put it: 'I would not be able to tell you the production schedules for the Fiesta in Genk or the Sierra in Cologne.'

More fundamentally the ability to co-operate is conditioned by the competition for new facilities among different plants, as the best means to protect employment. Where they could be said to be powerful enough to influence production decisions, the response of unions abroad to co-operation has largely been dominated by the wish to defend job opportunities in their own countries.

Several organizational factors have inhibited a stronger response. First, unions are nationally based for the most part and the international co-operation that has been developed is not comprehensive. Second, the multinational companies have resisted any efforts to establish international bargaining structures or even to co-ordinate the timing of bargaining between countries. Third, differences of interest and in structures and strategy have impeded the links between unions in different countries. For instance, British unions have found it difficult to sympathize with what has been called the co-operative strategy of German unionism (Marsden 1978), criticizing what they saw as their unquestioning acceptance of 'business criteria'; for example, the German metal workers union, I.G. Metall, has not opposed the internationalization of production in principle, accepting that this may be the only way for a firm to gain entry to a market on competitive terms, and that competitiveness is the key to employment security. In contrast, British unions have not accepted such arguments because their experience suggests the export of capital is a pretext for disinvestment and job loss. Second, ideological divisions within union movements, such as the Spanish, have inhibited the establishment of effective links. Third, differences in structure caused co-ordination difficulties: for instance, the lay organization in Britain was thought to be much stronger than in Germany. There, works councils operate at plant level, and are bound by legal frameworks governing their functions and the obligation to reach agreement without using sanctions. The dislocation of power centres between the two national systems has meant, in the view of the British full-time and lay officials, that it has been difficult to co-ordinate discussions because each side tended to liase with its equivalent level.

Overall, then, it appears that the impact of international unionism on the policies of the multinational producers has been marginal. Because these car producers have resisted international bargaining multinational unionism has remained retarded, but in addition differences of interest and differences in structure and in strategies have further impeded a more co-ordinated response.

Technical changes

Simultaneously with the internationalization of production, the trade unions have had to face the impact of microelectronic innovations to the production process, which as we saw in Chapter 3 have permitted extensive automation in certain areas. The unions' response to technical change has always been somewhat ambivalent. Their essential concern has been the labour displacement effects of automated processes and as Turner, Clack, and Roberts (1967) noted through the post-war period this question was a frequent source of disputes. Indeed one of the first major post-war strikes in the industry occurred nearly thirty years ago (in 1956) over redundancy caused by technical change. On the other hand, until the 1970s at least, fears of automation were offset by the increasing demand for labour made by the industry, and since the large scale shedding of labour began opposition to technical change has been muted because so few compulsory redundancies have directly resulted. Natural wastage, voluntary redundancy, and retraining have eased the position. Trade unions have also had to face the dilemma that in calling for high capital expenditure they may be endorsing the introduction of new processes and equipment, such as automated presses or engine machining lines, which displace their members. Hence technical change exposes the contradiction between short-term interests in preserving jobs and long-term interests in a competitive industry as the key to high employment. Union proposals have often skirted job displacement or productivity implications when calling for new investment, and in practice they have not resisted the introduction of new technical equipment. Rather, the general solution to automation now favoured by the British unions focuses on shorter working hours and the spreading of work. As we saw in Chapter 5, however, there has been resistance among the craft groups in particular to changes in the organization of work which might give semi-skilled workers access to what have been designated as skilled jobs.

Because its effects have thus far been uneven and remain to some extent undetermined technological change has also highlighted the difficulties for the unions in developing a coherent and unified strategy for change (Manwaring 1981). As Chapters 3 and 4 showed, the innovations have not simply meant a quantitive change in the labour force, but involved qualitative changes which represent an opportunity for some groups, and a threat to others.

The EETPU's members, for instance, face considerable opportunities for extending their job security and skills as long as they can control entry to and work on the increasing amount of microelectronically controlled equipment to maintain. Similarly, because of the accelerated rate of product innovation white-collar design technicians and engineers are becoming increasingly important and their function central to the achievement of competitive advantage. Their high demand has meant, for example, that their union, TASS, has been able to negotiate No Redundancy agreements with the three major firms in the UK, BL, Ford, and Vauxhall, and to enter into New Technology agreements giving considerable control over the innovation and use of CAD/CAM hardware. Moreover, the European integration of Ford and Vauxhall has already been resolved at the design stage and in the Ford's case now represents an advantage in terms of the amount of work. From an agreement negotiated in 1970 the Ford engineers have 60 per cent of Ford Europe's design work, and would be disadvantaged if the existing European basis of production was discontinued.

The prospects for the mechanical trades such as tool makers, pipe and machine tool fitters, and the pattern makers are more problematic. The tool makers, for instance, may face deskilling, becoming the machinists of design plans originated elsewhere (Jones 1982) or they may be able to shade their functions into those of the technicians and retain a bigger role in the design and production process.

In general, the uncertainty appears to have prompted alliances with stronger groups. The sheet metal workers have, for example, recently amalgamated with TASS and the pattern makers, whose jobs in prototype and experimental shops are threatened by the extension of CAE face a similar sort of decision. Partly this alliance of technician and craft has come about because of the experience of the tool-room trades who have consistently complained that the numerical predominance of the semi-skilled in the AUEW Engineering section has swamped their craft interests and led to an erosion of pay differentials. This issue prompted a series of major strikes at BL in the latter part of the 1970s which were as much against official union policy as against management. Considerable sympathy was shown by tool makers in each of the car firms and other skilled groups in the engineering sector including several components firms, and an industry-wide tool makers' committee was operational for a time, principally as a mode of exchanging information. In fact, each of the car firms experienced action by their tool makers in the 1970s. In response, however, the car firms have tried to offset separatist pressures by specifically accommodating craft interests in pay bargaining arrangements. At BL the solution developed following the revolts of the 1970s was to co-opt two craft representatives from the shop floor on to the AUEW delegation, but this still left them in a minority and therefore dissatisfied. Similarly, at Ford the gaining of representation rights on the

NJNC for lay craft representatives has not stemmed criticisms that the TGWU's dominance determines bargaining priorities.

There are, therefore, long-standing tensions between the crafts and the semi-skilled which are highlighted by the issue of technical change. In particular, the AUEW, which is now an all-grades union for the engineering sector, continues to face internal conflict between those skilled groups whose interests appear best served by the craft policy of 'closed' unionism, and its majority of semi-skilled members recruited since the union opened its ranks. If it cannot resolve this it will face the possibility of 'break-away' attempts resurfacing. This could prove particularly bitter if the craft groups such as the tool makers managed to align themselves with the other AUEW union TASS, the main technician union in the industry. Such developments would also intensify the existing political differences between the right-dominated engineers and the left-dominated TASS which have already created divisions on policies such as import controls.

For a combination of reasons, therefore, the response to technical change has been fragmented. Its effects have varied among different occupational groups and these have highlighted the sectionalism of British union structure in which unions tend to pursue particular aims and exclusive areas of control for their members. In this sense the traditional pursuit of 'job property rights', so often the cause of disputes in the past, has been intensified. It is notable that British unions have so far not been able to develop such thorough-going responses to the question of new technology as industrial unions in other countries. For instance, the German metal workers' union, I.G. Metall, has pursued policies which deal with change through the 'humanization of working life', including such proposals as the prohibition on work cycles of less than one and a half minutes and a general principle of pursuing job enrichment at the work-place but with limited success (Streeck and Hoff 1982). Similarly, in a major shift of policy in the US motor industry, the UAW has recently concentrated on getting agreement to retraining programmes for semi-skilled operatives in return for greater job security in its 1984 agreements with GM and Ford. This is not to say that the lack of bargaining about qualitative issues is entirely due to union disinterest.

What employers are prepared to talk about and negotiate on is also clearly of importance. It does appear, however, that the institutional divisions, plus an historical approach which focused on bargaining over the price of changes has inhibited the pooling of resources or ideas about longer-term policies on this broad subject.

Working practices

The changes to work organization have affected the basis of trade unionism in the car plants. Organizationally these developments have affected union representation in several ways. First, the breaking up of work groups has followed from the new flexibility and mobility of labour requirements. Such work groups were the basic cells of union organization on the shop floor in the past and regulated, through their steward, the customary levels of effort and manning on their respective sections. So not only did their break-up mean work-group solidarity was disturbed, it meant customary levels were more easily adjusted. In Chapter 5 we also saw that the role of stewards, the linchpins of plant organization, has been changed. Reductions in numbers have meant that in some plants, particularly Cowley, various sections were without representation at times. Nearly everywhere the new limits on the ability of stewards to leave their jobs has made it more difficult to pursue their representative role. Yet while these changes have weakened the traditional structures there has been no attempt to displace trade unions completely and new experiments such as teamworking (see Chapter 5) may offer the potential for new forms of work group to emerge around relatively stable teams, which with their close interdependence and work rotation theoretically form the basis of a solid organizational cell. It should also be added that there appears to have been considerable rank-and-file resistance, at least in the Cowley and Halewood assembly plants, to new labour mobility requirements.

Second, the car firms have all attempted to develop forms of employee involvement. Designed to shift the general emphasis away from the negotiation of change towards more collaborative methods, this has left the unions in a difficult predicament.

They seek to raise efficiency by drawing upon employees' views in problem-solving exercises, or at least create a closer understanding and identification with the company's situation and objectives. They therefore represent a clear move from the more adversarial approach of British unions and suspicion of any sort of participatory schemes as potentially divisive has usually prompted opposition both from the lay organizations and the national unions.

Yet if these schemes are seen by employees as means of obtaining greater job security, the trade union organizations run the risk of isolation from their members. For the car workers may be persuaded that co-operation is appropriate to achieve the productivity and quality standards which the intense competition in the industry requires, regardless of the union policy. In particular, the focus on quality through 'involvement' has been difficult to resist because, as one convenor pointed out, the visibility of most quality defects makes them difficult to dispute unless the plant is worn out. But also from the point of view of rejuvenating shop-floor organization a number of stewards and full-time officials have seen some advantages in exploring more co-operative strategies. Even though part of a management strategy, consultative structures could be 'tapped' to remobilize rank-and-file activity, to overcome the apathy and fatalism that weakened work-place organization. Participation could also be used to galvanize interest in a broader range of issues than the typical 'bread and butter' questions. This sort of thinking appears to underpin the strategy of the UAW in the USA in conceding greater flexibility and co-operation in return for unprecedented commitments to retraining and job security. In effect, the American union has conceded that the unprecedented product market competition can only be met by a highly co-operative labour strategy, particularly if the industry is to try and match Japanese standards. As yet this has not become part of the British unions bargaining strategy, but in future 'co-operation' in various guises may become more favoured. Partly, this may be in acquiescence to management pressure but partly as well because it is seen to have certain advantages for the shop-floor organizations as a strategy, given that the only alternative currently proposed presupposes a sympathetic Labour government committed to planning agreements and high public funding.

Political solutions

It can be seen, then, that the traditional bargaining strategies of the car workers have failed to provide a means of controlling the changes in the organization of the industry. Unions have been unclear about their response and divisions between rank-and-file members, lay officials, and national leaders have impeded a consistent challenge to management strategies. Recognizing these shortcomings the unions have recently (and perhaps belatedly) turned to political means of regulating the competitive conditions facing the car industry to safeguard their members' interests.

First widely publicized in 1979, the content and timing of these political solutions reflected the preoccupation of the trade unions with BL. For although in calling for import controls they expressed a concern about the growth in tied imports among the British-based foreign companies, the main thrust of the proposals was to protect a weakening BL at a time when its market share was falling to an unprecedented low point. This central concern with BL reflected its distinctive status as the only British-owned company and its public ownership. But such a concern was arguably one reason why the response of the trade unions to the internationalization of the industry was relatively belated: until the 1979 crisis the unions had held faith with the expansion plans of Ryder, by which BL was to become the dominant firm in the British motor industry. They therefore did not foresee the impact on jobs of the structural changes occurring in the foreign-owned firms.

When we considered the trade union response to Ford's decision to integrate its European production the other reason for this relatively belated response was identified. It was the plant-based unions which led the initiatives on these issues rather than the national unions, in keeping with the traditionally decentralized policies in the industry. Only with the collapse of BL's markets and its contraction in size were industry-wide proposals developed. Those then put forward from the TGWU, TASS, and the engineering union, were given support by an independent study of BL by the consulting group Eurofinance. Assessing BL's chances of survival in the medium term (to 1985) as relatively weak, the report concluded that import controls would be a desirable option for the company, at least in the short term, because they would reduce foreign supplies from its British-based competitors and place it in a better position to reach advantageous collaborative deals with other would-be importers. Over the longer term, the prospects for BL were still argued to be poor without external support, because it was not big enough to achieve the economies of scale in production. This reinforced the argument for special assistance measures from the state.

Subsequently, broader proposals from the TUC (representing the motor industry unions) and the Labour Party have been put forward. Each has to be seen as a part of Labour's reflationary strategy for the whole economy, and common to both is the objective of rebuilding output and employment in the British motor industry through government intervention. At its height in the late 1960s, with production in excess of 1.5 million units, over half a million people were directly employed in the industry, virtually double existing levels. Today, automation and higher productivity would reduce the unemployment at comparable outputs, nevertheless through substantial (but unspecified) public funding the intention is to create continuously high demand for British vehicles in the home market as the means of expanding employment. This would be complemented by raising exports, particularly to Western Europe, through the mechanism of adjusting the sterling exchange rate. In these later proposals import controls have not been abandoned, but have become a sanction of last resort. Instead the proposed mechanism for controlling the multinationals is a series of voluntary planned-production agreements with each of the British-based firms to achieve orderly marketing arrangements. In this way it is hoped to overcome the insecurity of employment which characterized the industry even in the long boom period.

Clearly, the central weakness of these proposals is their political contingency. Without a Labour government, the unions remain without an operational strategy for the industry. Generally, in fact, their influence through tripartite bodies such as NEDO is minimal and has been throughout the crisis period. This was partly because the major unions relied on the personal influence of their general secretaries to represent their views in NEDO in the 1970s rather than on institutional lines and there is still no Economic Development Council in NEDO specifically for the motor industry. But even if one was established, it is unlikely that much could be achieved as there is little basis for consensus between employers and unions on how to tackle the industry's problems. Furthermore, even with a future Labour administration, doubts must be raised about how much could be achieved in the lifetime of one government, first if the multinationals chose to stall rather than co-operate, and second given the long-term planning horizons under which capital investment decisions are made.

CONCLUSIONS

Labour performance became critical to the British motor industry in the 1970s, when the manufacturers found themselves lagging behind not only the Japanese competitors but West European standards. This prompted strong efforts to reform the patterns of work organization and to reduce the resistance of the work-force to changes; they were accompanied by strategies designed to weaken or constrain shop-floor union organization. These strategies were successful in so far as higher productivity levels were imposed, labour was shed relatively easily, and unit labour costs were reduced as pay was, for the most part, linked more closely to output.

Why were the car firms so successful? How were such changes been achieved in the face of a trade union organization that had developed a reputation for militancy and successfully challenging managerial controls? Examining the growth of trade union in the car industry we saw they had traditionally been based within the plants and around individual work groups, with shop stewards as the key bargaining representatives. These groups established job controls from which they could bargain with managers over any proposed changes. The official union structure was thus relatively unimportant except to fix basic rates in national negotiations. This decentralism was suited to the expansionary period of the industry after the war as a way to maximize the opportunities presented for wage increases, but proved to be less effective in the face of the greater competitive pressures facing the car firms and the centralization of management controls.

In particular, plant-based unionism proved vulnerable to a variety of managerial strategies. At BL these explicitly divided the rank and file from the shop steward organization while co-opting the national union officials to support or accept closures and tighter discipline. In the context of high losses BL's measures exposed the key dilemma facing workers, stewards, and national officials. This was whether to resist change and risk bankruptcy with massive job losses or to accept certain changes to increase the probability of survival, even though this substantially weakened the basis of union organization and involved some reduction in the size of the firm anyway. Loss-making in Talbot and Vauxhall forced workers there into similar decisions. At Ford, the company's profitability allowed a stronger challenge to managerial control to be maintained; but in all of the foreign firms the internationalization of production provided a further dimension to the dilemma facing the shop floor. For, on the threat of disinvestment each firm was able to demand that its British workers match European production standards and to reassert management control through the dissolution of customary working practices.

In contesting the internationalization of motor manufacture some union actions appeared to have limited success. Campaigns such as the S-car dispute at Vauxhall in 1983 suggested, however, that the car workers would require the assistance of other groups, notably dock workers and other transport staff, to be effective. This demonstrated the strength of one British form of unionism, the general union as characterized by the TGWU, to confront international production.

On the other hand, the technical innovations based on micro-electronic processes introduced over the last decade appear to have further divided the unions. In looking at how they had confronted new technology we saw that divisions of interests between different occupational groups had been exposed and reinforced by institutional divisions between various unions. The British union structure thus impeded a more co-ordinated response. This issue also illustrated the basic dilemma facing labour, that it cannot resist change too strongly in so far as automation is central to competitiveness and thus to improving the chances of a firm's survival, even though labour is displaced by new technologies.

We can conclude, then, that trade union organization has been profoundly affected by the changes to the industry in the 1970s. In the USA, where the car industry experienced similar difficulties, we noted that the UAW union has chosen recently to adopt more co-operative policies through 'concession bargaining' with the American firms in return for new commitment to job security. Thus far the British unions have generally declined to try and imitate this sort of approach, and expressed suspicion towards efforts by the British firms to implement employee involvement schemes. Instead the emphasis has switched to more political strategies. We argued that although in the mid-1970s it proved possible for the unions to use political pressure in influencing sourcing decisions, with a less sympathetic Conservative government this became no longer feasible. The decision to develop political strategies to counter the problems caused by multinational sourcing and strong foreign competition was also seen to be somewhat belated. None the less, starting with a preference for import controls, the central strategy of the national unions is now explicitly political in so far as it relies upon a Labour government to operate a series of planning agreements in the motor industry, supported by public funding and exchange rate management to expand British car output. Without a Labour government, however, there is no coordinated union strategy for the industry and the car workers remain without a unified alternative to the prospect of intense international competition and the continuing drive to improve production efficiency.

EIGHT
CONCLUSIONS

INTRODUCTION

In the late 1970s, many plants in the British car industry were typical of the 'British disease' with low productivity, poor quality, inadequate control of labour costs, and weak management. They were often also characterized by powerful shop steward organizations and shop-floor militancy. But between 1979 and 1984 a series of major changes took place with the introduction of new models, new technology, changed working practices, and increased management control. By 1984, BL could claim that Longbridge was the most efficient plant in Europe, and Ford and Vauxhall could claim that certain parts of their operations and certain plants (not Halewood) had, for similar technology, greatly reduced the efficiency gap with West Germany.

A number of questions arise. How have the industrial relations changes contributed to improved efficiency and productivity? What do such changes tell us about the role of industrial relations in an industry's economic performance; and how have the changes affected the position of the unions? Finally, are the changes likely to be durable, or will they be reversed in the near future? We shall look at these questions in this final chapter.

THE ROLE OF INDUSTRIAL RELATIONS

There has been some considerable debate about the extent to which the manifest competitive disadvantage experienced by the UK car industry has its roots in 'bad' industrial relations. As far back as the 1960s the Donovan Commission suggested that unofficial strikes, restrictions on labour utilization, and problems emerging from the use of payment by results caused such a disadvantage: the car industry was their principal case. Reviews of productivity-inhibiting labour relations factors in the UK in the 1970s similarly focused upon the motor industry as an exemplar of several forms of 'bad' practice (Batstone 1984: 122–80).

Most recently, the publicly expressed views of the manufacturers themselves – particularly Ford and BL – explain poor UK performance at least partly in these terms. However, a number of problems arise. The Donovan view may not have been too accurate a picture of the car industry even at the time. After all, Turner's theory of strikes as mechanisms for dealing with surplus labour in the short term contradicts the view that strikes would have a straightforwardly depressive affect upon productivity in the industry. Despite being influenced by other parts of Turner's analysis, the Report plays down this aspect of industrial conflict. In any case, the Donovan prescriptions pointed to defects in labour relations institutions which had been largely removed by the reform of bargaining at BL prior to 1979. Moreover, these institutional defects only became serious in the context of relatively buoyant product markets in which cost considerations were secondary to maintaining production. The product market changes described in Chapter 2 point to the existence of substantial over-capacity in Europe after 1979 which might generate a very different view of manufacturer's labour relations requirements. In short, in evaluating the impact of labour relations on competitiveness between 1979 and 1985, one must take account of substantial changes not only to industrial relations institutions but also to processes and product markets.

As we noted in Chapter 3, the retooling exercises have emphasized the need for continuity of production: this 'process' logic requires that the cost of capital investment be spread over a manufacturer's entire productive capacity and puts a premium upon the avoidance of increasingly costly machine downtime. Forms of work organization or labour relations which restrict or interrupt output are thus, *ceteris paribus*, undesirable for managers. However, there are at least two other sets of considerations. Because of the poor or deteriorating competitive position of the UK manufacturers between 1979 and 1984 considerable pressures emerged to control costs: although labour costs may have varied as a percentage of total costs between manufacturers, they always represent a substantial proportion. This cost consideration meant that one possible solution to the problem of production continuity – namely retention of an inefficiently organized labour force to provide cover for the avoidance of interruptions – was ruled out. It ruled out paying higher wages for the acceptance of change.

Together, then, improvements in process and costs required the reduction and reorganization of the car industry labour force at progressively lower real earnings levels. Any firm which could not effect this reduction and reorganization would, *ceteris paribus*, suffer from a unit cost disadvantage determined both by the extent of the failure of labour reform and the scale and market position of operations.

However, this is not yet the whole story, since the requirement to compete in a changing product market imposed occasionally contradictory pressures. The most obvious stems from the renewed emphasis on quality and product performance. The use of automated techniques and the advent of Japanese competition served during the 1970s to highlight the relatively poor quality of the products of the UK industry, and while the adoption of automated techniques by the UK industry could in part remedy the problem, full solutions required improving the quality of labour input. At least two solutions were possible. One relied on the intensive monitoring of the quality of labour input and product output through increased numbers of supervisors and inspectors. However, this was a much more expensive option than the second, which consisted of the attempt to involve employees in a concern for product quality through self-inspection of work and various consultative devices. In the pursuit of this second option, UK manufacturers have explicitly sought to remove what they see as one comparative advantage of the Japanese industry. Once more, any company which fails to secure such gains will experience either the higher manufacturing costs of more inspection or loss of sales through poor quality.

Overall, then, strikes, restrictions on labour utilization or the failure to secure sufficient co-operation from a work-force can all generate competitive disadvantage, but assessment of the extent of disadvantage at any point in time is extremely difficult for any one manufacturer, much less the UK industry as a whole. The reasons for this emerge from the discussions of Chapter 6. The *production* loss experienced in the course of a particular dispute depends not only on its size, duration, and location in the production process but also on production schedules, which in turn vary both between model lines and seasonally. But the cost of a dispute must include revenue loss, which in turn also depends upon season and the level of existing stocks, as well as upon the extent to which lost production can be made up *after* the dispute in order to prevent loss of sales. The complexity of these considerations helps to explain why there is no simple relationship between working days lost and production losses.

The costs of particular restrictive practices may be related to slightly different considerations. In the removal of 'early finishing' in 1983, Austin Rover management made quite precise calculations of cost increases and potential revenue loss in Maestro production, but events after the return to work revealed that such calculations were not relevant to other product lines. In a similar way, the costs of a variety of restrictive practices at Halewood appear in higher levels of man-hours per car, and thus higher unit costs. Inefficient forms of labour utilization may thus provide a constant impediment to competitiveness – on the assumption that price is important and that the costs of restrictive labour practices can no longer be transmitted to the consumer – which affects periods both of relatively high and low demand.

The persistence of demand fluctuations does however raise once more the question of possible benefits arising from strikes and restrictive practices. Under certain circumstances, particularly where supplier strikes such as the 1984 I.G. Metall dispute are involved, or where unexpected market slumps cause expensive stockpiling, it costs manufacturers less to experience a strike than to lay-off. The benefits here need not be restricted to savings in wages, energy costs, and the like if the opportunity is taken to press bargaining advantage to resolve other outstanding items in the course of the dispute. In such circumstances, car manufacturers' quotations of the costs of production losses may have no counterpart in sales loss, while other explicit condemnations of a dispute may have less to do with the immediate search for resolution and more to do with an ideological struggle between management and unions.

Similarly, restrictive practices may be tolerated as a form of work-sharing. In the UK, this is probably no longer widespread on direct work, but as yet no UK manufacturer has effected thorough-going reform of the system of craft demarcations on maintenance work. While undoubtedly reflecting the power of craftsmen to maintain some controls over manning levels, persistence of demarcation may also serve managerial goals.

In summary, then, industrial relations issues can effect competitive success in a number of different ways. In the first instance, poor industrial relations may impose a cost penalty on manufacturers either by causing a gap between actual and scheduled output (through strikes) or by raising the unit costs of scheduled output (through overmanning). However, given the importance of product quality, good industrial relations may provide certain benefits: successful employee involvement exercises may be a cheap way of obtaining quality improvement and cost reduction. Finally, these considerations are complicated by the potential for manipulative behaviour on the part of manufacturers wishing to reduce costs or push through changes where consequential loss of revenue is small or unlikely.

These factors explain the reforms of the period 1979–84. Overall, increased competitive pressure in the product market has been of greatest importance. The UK producers felt the need to launch new models of higher quality at the lowest possible cost. Process innovations may be understood primarily in terms of these cost and quality considerations. Similarly, labour relations reform is governed by cost and quality considerations complicated by the impact of process change upon the demand for skill and manpower: the details of change may be understood in terms of the requirement to secure supplies of appropriately qualified labour to reduce labour costs and remove the ability of trade unions to interfere with the productive process while maximizing individual employee commitment to product quality. It is thus central to the argument here that while the capacity of managers to effect labour relations changes was enhanced by rapidly rising unemployment rates, the purpose of these changes was not merely to take advantage of suddenly slack labour markets but rather to secure certain product market objectives. Since this clearly has a bearing on the durability of labour relations change, we shall return to this argument below.

Given the argument so far, the first point to emphasize is that many of the labour relations changes in the UK car industry have been the result of *strategic* decisions: since a number of authors have encouraged caution in the use of this term, it is useful to clarify what is meant at the outset. Here, the term is not used simply to suggest that the changes we have noted resulted from board level decisions about the development of personnel and industrial relations matters in the medium term. Rather, changes to labour relations matters were decided at the highest level as part of a broader competitive strategy upon which they were premised. The example of the two largest UK producers may be quoted here. At Ford, the 'After Japan' campaign implied the reform of work organization and employment reductions, but only as necessary prerequisites for the achievement of the specific targets on market penetration, return on investment, and internal economies. At BL, the parameters of change laid out in the 1980 'Blue Newspaper' related directly to prior decisions about investment in new technology and new products which comprised the 'product-led recovery'.

Moreover, although we can argue that reforms at BL were more fundamental because the company felt it had much further to travel in order to reach competitive levels of productivity, the parameters of shop-floor reform were similar in kind if different in degree. As one might expect, following the discussion of the previous section, the emphasis in both cases was on the reassertion of the right to manage, the reduction of direct labour input, and the attempt to encourage employee involvement.

This convergence of strategy raises a number of interesting

questions. Some writers have suggested that the most successful post-war labour relations strategy in the car industry – and for that matter in other mass production industries – can be characterized as 'Fordism', the elements of which are the fragmentation of individual work tasks, close supervision of machine-paced work, an associated emphasis on the right to manage, and the payment of high day-rates (Lewchuck 1983; Sable 1982). Lewchuck in fact suggests that events at BL in the late 1970s can be characterized as an attempt to emulate 'Fordism', the move to measured day-work having been a largely unsuccessful prelude (1984). The extent of this convergence on a particular strategy merits further discussion.

All of the UK producers have used the two principles of machine pacing and task fragmentation at least since World War II, hence if convergence in these areas occurred, it probably followed from innovation diffusion some time ago. However, the associated question of the relationship between technology and work organization remains relevant. Despite extensive retooling and market changes in the early 1980s, no UK manufacturer has moved away from these two principles, although a number of writers (e.g. Sabel 1982) have argued that microelectronic technology allows for extensive task and product differentation. The question then arises: has work organization on automated assembly systems followed from technological imperatives or from managerial choice?

As a caveat at the outset, two points are worth making. First, trim and final assembly operations are left largely unchanged. Second, car assembly had proceeded for some years prior to automation at firms such as Volvo without direct machine pacing, and these systems have survived the advent of robotic body assembly. One ought not therefore to suggest too extensive a set of possibilities for work reorganization arising out of technical change *per se*, and it seems reasonable to conclude that assembly-line techniques remain the most efficient means of producing at high volumes. Once this has been admitted, the trends observed in Chapter 4, and predicted by Abernathy (1978), seem likely to continue for the future: namely the progressive reduction of numbers of direct workers without removal of fragmentation of remaining jobs, and the increasing relative numerical importance of highly skilled maintenance technicians. In the absence of possibilities for internal promotion, the progressive polarization of skilled and unskilled tasks may occur.

However, at this point it is worth emphasizing the available degrees of freedom in the organization of direct work, not least because the process technologies in use in the UK vary. Automated assembly has tended to proceed via removal of the simplest and most unpleasant tasks, often those where quality has been most variable. Those direct jobs which remain can be performed in a number of ways. For example, teamwork such as that at BL allows for job rotation: the provision of magazine loading or the insertion of small buffer stocks may allow for wider mobility between jobs, although it is worth recalling from Chapter 6 that such mobility may not be welcomed by employees if it represents mere redeployment and contains no element of job progression.

This raises two further points. Even if one starts from the existence of a given arrangement of production equipment, implying a set of maintenance concerns and a residual set of direct labour operations, two issues arise concerning *mobility* and *progression*, and here more similarities emerge in the strategies of UK producers. Put briefly, all the UK producers rely on managerial authority to determine mobility between jobs, and none have moved towards career progression for manual workers across the craft divide (see Chapters 4 and 5). In Ford, the re-establishment of managerial authority required merely the enforcement of existing agreements. At BL it required the removal of mutuality and the introduction of a pivotal role for supervisors in the control of zone working. But both companies have avoided a head-on assault on craft privilege. In both cases and for both issues, the resulting organization of work has more to do with managerial choice than with technological determination.

Overall, it is tempting to conclude that, to the extent that the UK producers pursue Fordism, they do so on the basis of their common interpretation of the requirements of producing cars for the mass market under competitive conditions. Moreover, to the extent that their labour relations strategies, either individually or collectively, diverge from Fordism, product market conditions are important. Two areas are relevant here: first, the reliance on bonus payments by companies other than Ford; second, the general concern with employee involvement exercises. We shall deal with each in turn.

Between 1979 and 1982 bonus earnings became important in the constituent plants of BL, Talbot, and Vauxhall, while Ford retained its day-rate policy. Since, as we have noted, most work is either indirect or machine paced, and the bonus schemes are operated at plant level, divorced from individual effort input, their logic is, at first sight, difficult to discern. By contrast, the Ford policy of securing labour supply through relatively high stable earnings and output through managerial control is clear. The policies of the other manufacturers may be seen in several different ways. Bonus payments which vary with accurately measured output may reveal the experience of product-market uncertainty and a willingness to transmit it to employees in the form of variable earnings. Bonus schemes may also illustrate a lack of faith in the capacity of managers, particularly first-line supervisors, to secure acceptable output through discipline alone. However, a third view, accepted particularly by managers at Austin Rover, is that bonus schemes may facilitate the acceptance of change: improvements in the efficiency of labour utilization or reductions in manpower at constant output both lead to earnings increase. The schemes thus do not remove productivity improvements entirely from the negotiating arena: at Austin Rover, for example, bonus is consolidated in the biennial pay reviews, even though it is not negotiable at plant level. At GM also, annual pay reviews involve bargaining over efficiency improvements. By contrast, at Ford, work loads and productivity are entirely managerial responsibilities.

The final area to consider is that of employee involvement. The concern on the part of employers for consultative or involvement exercises tends to be recurrent: employers generally want help when they are in trouble and ignore employee influence when they are not, hence the pursuit of participation tends to be akin to the pursuit of companionship in distress. However, valid though this view may be, it should not trivialize the pursuit of employee involvement in the car industry since 1979. On the one hand, it is a response to very specific product market features, on the other it does involve a development away from Fordism pure and simple.

The concern for employee involvement exercises emerged in the late 1970s directly from a concern with non-price Japanese competition. In the USA at Ford and GM too significant progress in developing employee involvement institutions has been made. Reliability and quality features of Japanese exports were seen to follow in part from the success of such mechanisms as quality circles in encouraging employee concern with product quality but without direct financial incentives to do so. The imitation of these mechanisms – or some having similarly low costs and success – was seen as necessary, but not all UK producers were able to change the labour relations climate effectively. As we showed in Chapter 4, firms with a history of good labour relations, such as Jaguar and Vauxhall, tended to be more successful: by contrast consultation has been much less successful in the largely adversarial climates of Ford and BL, despite both companies' concern to promote involvement.

The importance of the latest phase of involvement exercises is enhanced rather than diminished by the recognition that they are product-orientated rather than being concerned with participation or employee satisfaction *per se*. Undoubtedly the prime concern of UK manufacturers has been with efficiency gains which follow from high levels of motivation among manual workers, but this has been sought in the absence of the provision of several 'props' for the success of such exercises.

To the extent, then, that involvement exercises persist and succeed, a more sophisticated labour relations strategy has developed among UK producers. Whereas in the past they sought to minimize employee's power to stop production, now they seek in addition to exploit the benefits of untapped employee potential. However, to date, UK producers are characterized by a generally ambivalent view of labour as a cost on the one hand and as a resource on the other.

THE UNION RESPONSE

The response from trade unions to these strategic initiatives has been discussed in the previous chapter. Once the reliance on shop-floor power was no longer viable, union policies focused rather less on the car manufacturers themselves and rather more on the prospects of political intervention to influence corporate behaviour, either directly or through suspension of those competitive conditions that allowed 'harder' management styles to succeed. Two implications are of particular interest – the role of collective bargaining in a recession and the role of shop stewards in the industry.

The failure of the unions in the industry to prevent progressive loss of employment and deterioration of the earnings position of the industry over the last half decade may be seen as testament to the inability of collective bargaining mechanisms to protect employment and earnings in adverse economic circumstances. In defence of the union position, it does need to be said that, despite technological change, employment in Ford and BL fell less rapidly than did output over much of the period 1979–82; unions may thus argue that they delayed job losses. Moreover, small comfort to the unions though it may be, no company has yet sought either to withdraw recognition from unions or to open non-union greenfield sites, despite the fact that Nissan and GM did so in the USA.

Indeed, the collective bargaining preferences of the companies do seem to point to the development of a system of industrial relations in the industry which in some ways parallels that in the USA: relatively long-term, comprehensive agreements are currently preferred which clearly separate the making of joint rules from their administration, by institutionalizing a division between consultation in the plants and negotiation at company level. Overall, the frequency of bargaining has been drastically reduced.

Given that the pattern of management–union relations in the USA are in a state of flux, it is probably wise not to press this comparison too far, but there are two features of recent collective bargaining developments in the USA that do appear relevant given the discussions of the previous section. These are concerns with employee involvement and job security (often in the context of concession bargaining) which appear to have been rather more central to negotiations there than here (Katz 1984).

The lack of attention paid by British trade unions to the task of securing job security guarantees and their resistance to involvement probably both have their history in the reliance on decentralized bargaining. For many years, stewards could protect jobs through bargaining power in the context of an essentially adversarial relationship with management. Then, rather suddenly, they could not. But it can be argued that job guarantees may become important in the future, and that it is an area where progress can be made given the current concerns of managers and the position of trade unions.

The question of redundancies may be raised again once Nissan opens up its plant in the North-East. Then, unless the UK market expands, or export performance improves, there will be greater over-capacity than at present. As we have noted, it is already rather easier to effect redundancies in the UK than in several other European countries, and the absence of any clear stratification between native and immigrant work-forces makes it less easy to separate secure and insecure sections of the industry's work-force. Moreover, the unions have been unable to resist past redundancies in the absence of employment guarantees. They may seek some improvement in employment protection in future.

On the other hand, some concessions may be forthcoming. Despite their weakened position, unions look likely to retain almost 100 per cent membership in the industry for the foreseeable future. Despite the relative failure of the 1984 pay dispute at Austin Rover, strikes organized at Ford, Jaguar, and Vauxhall secured further concessions from management, indicating that bargaining power is still present. Most significantly, the concern with consultation and involvement on the part of employers implies that the work-force, or at least part of it, retains something to bargain with. While cost-conscious managers are unlikely to concede high wage rises given the financial state of the UK industry, quality-conscious ones may be prepared to follow through the logic of involvement exercises. Some trade-off of job security for improved productivity has already been made in other countries (Katz 1985; Streeck 1984).

The final issue concerns the role of shop stewards in the industry. Chapter 5 described the different experience of stewards in the main manufacturers: throughout the industry, but particularly in BL, the period since 1979 has seen a reduction in steward numbers and facilities, and an almost complete removal of their ability to bargain at or below plant level. Given Turner's famous dictum that 'the steward is the union' in the car industry in the 1960s, changes in steward power are central to considerations of employee bargaining power. However, in assessing the significance of the so-called 'roll-back' of steward organization since 1979, several points need to be borne in mind.

The first is that, although a reduction in facilities, numbers, and the range of bargaining activity for stewards occured at the end of the decade, it appears to have been the case that expansion occurred in all three areas during the 1970s. This expansion in steward activity in the industry was in keeping with developments elsewhere in manufacturing (Batstone 1984). As a consequence, steward influence may not be substantially weaker with either managers or employees than it was in the late 1960s. Certainly, the wheel has not turned full circle and there is no immediate sign of a return to the circumstances of the early 1950s when steward organization in the major car plants was virtually non-existent (Tolliday and Zeitlin 1982).

Currently, the state of shop steward organization at Ford and Vauxhall appears, under the circumstances, to have changed relatively little. At Jaguar and at Austin Rover's Longbridge plant fewer stewards with lesser facilities nevertheless felt that their organization was intact. By contrast, the most severe reversals appear to have been experienced at Cowley assembly plant.

In fact, it is important not to generalize from events at BL, where the change in steward influence was most substantial, and the situation most untypical. From being involved in joint management of BL in 1977, stewards were excluded even from consultative exercises in 1980. However, the position since then has reversed somewhat, and in any case, the position of stewards at BL in the 1970s may have appeared stronger than in fact it was. Involvement in participation may have been a substantial disadvantage for stewards who were seen by members to be too deeply involved in the difficulties faced by the company to command employee support in opposition to the Edwardes's plan.

An important question thus concerns the role of generally

intact steward organizations in the absence of any ability to negotiate over pay or work organization. As Terry (1983) notes more generally it is unlikely, given the problems of dealing with sectional work-group action, that companies would seek to destroy the representative structures altogether. Moreover, the success of consultative or involvement exercises depends upon the establishment of some form of structure which is seen as legitimate by employees: hence, at Jaguar, the convenor is closely involved with quality circle activities, while at Austin Rover, the consultative machinery of the 1982 procedure builds explicitly on existing collective bargaining and involves shop stewards. In the same company, the problems which arise when a shop steward organization becomes debilitated beyond the point where control of the membership is possible could be seen in the events of 1984 at Cowley assembly plant described in Chapter 6.

For a number of reasons, deeper steward involvement in consultative arrangements in the future is highly likely. First, the emphasis on rigid adherence to procedure and 'constitutional' trade unionism effectively rules out a great range of other activities. Second, if the above argument is correct, and job security concerns become more prominent in the future, then access to company information including new product development, production schedules, and manpower projections will prove essential. This involves rather more than manager–shop steward relations. The employee involvement exercises involve giving a great deal of information directly to employees who, if they wish, may thus become more knowledgeable about both company and product. If stewards are to retain some authority in the eyes of employees, then the use of relatively privileged access to managerial personnel and documentation may be essential: consultation is, at the moment, the stewards' principal resource and collective bargaining alone has not proved too successful in the recent past.

PROSPECTS FOR THE FUTURE

The central question for the future concerns the durability of the industrial relations changes effected between 1979 and 1985.

Since these changes were pushed through in the face of mounting product market difficulties and against a background of rapidly rising unemployment, one might question the effects on the new regime of managerial authority, changed working practices, and labour efficiency of more buoyant product markets and tighter labour markets. Put simply, can the unions recoup lost ground in the future?

If this recovery were to involve a return to the circumstances of the 1970s, then its likelihood varies between companies. For example, for BL to return to the circumstances of the late 1970s would require not only a return to decentralized bargaining via further reform of industrial relations institutions, but also the re-establishment of mutuality. The latter reversal would imply the removal of the entire managerial philosophy established by Michael Edwardes. At Ford, less change would be required. A return to the sort of local steward influence of the early 1970s would require little institutional change, but instead the power to exert influence on local management practice. However, even here there has been change to local management discretion that would make such managerial concession less likely if they served to raise costs or inhibit productivity. The 'After Japan' approach in effect provides a centralized control in this area: by setting quality, cost, and break-even standards it places plant performance within a strategic setting such that the costs of concession may be experienced in redundancy or plant closure in the short term.

An important qualitative change in the UK producers has thus been the establishment of more rigorous and more sophisticated cost control systems by managers which make the re-establishment of local shop-floor controls by shop stewards less likely, even given favourable economic circumstances. Were product or labour market conditions to improve, a much more likely development than 'old-style' shop steward control would be some form of productivity-based bargaining, given that labour costs and productivity are still low by international standards. Given that reductions in direct worker employment have been proportionately much greater than in indirect areas, and given that the UK producers retain relatively high levels of maintenance employment in part because craft organization persists, one area for such bargaining might be that of skilled craft employment. The potential for such a development is raised by the relative shortage of highly skilled employees: should demand for them increase, bottlenecks to output expansion and to earnings increases might be removed by such an approach. Nevertheless, managers in the major companies are now highly aware of the cost of making piecemeal concessions on principles in order to keep production moving.

However, there seems little prospect of a rapid and sustained expansion in the market for UK-produced cars. Within the UK, expansion of new car demand is slow, governed by a three- to four-year replacement cycle which implies that 1983 levels of demand may not be reached again until 1988. The propensity of the market to suck in imports is unlikely to be reduced unless government action or exchange rate movements act to raise the price of imported cars. In the export markets too there is little prospect of rapid expansion. The most rapid areas of global sales growth are in the Third World and the USA, to which UK producers tend not to have access. By contrast, the major export markets for UK cars are in Western Europe, which currently has massive over-capacity, and in relatively unstable markets such as South Africa (receiving approximately 20 per cent of UK exports in 1984) and Iran (10 per cent).

Government action could, of course, affect both product and labour markets. Reflation of the UK economy might lead to tighter labour markets and higher labour costs as well as higher levels of demand for cars: restrictions on imports could assist higher levels of production in the UK. This would, of course, affect producers unevenly if it restricted the ability of GM and Ford to maintain the current levels of tied imports or if government assistance directly to Austin Rover were thought appropriate. However, unless government action in the future went so far as to insulate the UK industry both from its primary export market and its most severe competitors, both of which are in Western Europe, any assistance to the re-emergence of any shop-floor controls would put the UK at a competitive disadvantage.

One of the problems for UK unions dealing with multinational producers is the threat of disinvestment. Over the period, GM and Peugeot Citroen have reduced their UK capacity. In GM

cessation of engine production *and* the retooling of Ellesmere
Port have both been linked to industrial relations performance.
Ford have continued to expand their UK operations but poor
labour relations at Halewood assembly operation have allegedly
jeopardized the company's commitment to future investment
there. In bargaining with any of these companies, unions
constantly face comparisons with productivity levels of overseas
producers and the prospect that strike action or productivity
restriction will lead either to disinvestment or a failure to
attract future investment. Given the history of labour relations
in the UK car industry and the continued presence of major
manufacturers, one could argue that such prospects are illusory.
However, once more product market changes are important,
and the existence of over-capacity in Western Europe at a time
of rapid innovation makes for a period of relatively rapid shift
in investment in productive capacity within a company. The
attraction of low-wage UK for location of new plants is lost if
low productivity nevertheless raises unit costs.

Having said this, the prospects for further investment in the
UK by major producers look good in the short term. Jaguar
and Austin Rover can currently scarcely locate elsewhere, but
all of the foreign and subsidiaries intend further UK investment.
In 1984, Ford announced plans to invest over £75 million in
paint facilities and gearbox production at Halewood, where
Ghia versions of the Escort and Orion, previously sourced
from West Germany, are to be produced. In the period to 1988,
GM is committed to spending £260 million at Luton and
Ellesmere Port, the biggest element involving modernized paint
facilities at both plants. More modestly, Talbot plan to invest
£20 million to modernize Ryton to assemble a new range of
cars. Against these figures must be set the decisions to restrict
or transfer operations from the UK in the past five years, but
they do indicate a general commitment to UK production.

Moreover, during the 1980s, the UK will acquire another
major assembly operation when Nissan open in the North-
East. This may have several significant consequences. At
present, Nissan is the major importer into the UK, with about
6 per cent of the UK market over the period 1979–84.
Presumably, such imports will be reduced once the UK operation
opens, but it still seems likely that this will further fragment

the UK market, and that employment growth at Nissan may have to be offset against losses elsewhere unless there is compensatory export growth: on the basis of recent performance, employment seems safer at GM, Jaguar, and Ford than at Talbot and Austin Rover.

For trade unions, the blessings of such investments may appear mixed. On the one hand, the UK industry has little future without them. On the other, new plant is likely to accelerate the growth of labour productivity which, in the absence of major output expansion, will continue to erode employment levels in the industry. Moreover, new factories and new product lines are unlikely to provide a congenial environment for the growth of shop-floor organization, both because companies may not select employees for these lines who have a record of union activity and because lower manning and extensive redeployment associated with newer lines may prevent the formation of stable and cohesive work groups.

In short, it is difficult to envisage the development in the short to medium term of economic conditions which might sustain the re-establishment of local bargaining power. It is even more difficult to imagine the sorts of organizational changes within car companies which would support it. However, other changes that trade unions might regard as beneficial reversals of recent trends might occur. In order to understand the basis for this, one must return again to company perceptions of the product market and the development or initiation of strategies to succeed in it.

The UK producers have in fact tended to borrow much of their labour relations strategy from abroad. Ford explicitly follow Japan with the 'After Japan' campaign, Vauxhall follow the lead of GM in the USA, and Austin Rover emulate West European competitors. In all cases the strategy involves some mix of efficient manufacturing policy which requires the removal of any trade union influence and the attempts at employee involvement that require the maintenance of some form of collective organization amongst employees. Cost and quality considerations are the parameters for its retention. The models for the strategies which UK producers have initiated display a number of advantages for trade unions: specifically operations implementing these strategies in Japan, Europe, and the USA pay higher wages, offer greater job security guarantees, and encourage greater employee involvement than their UK counterparts. Such benefits are not necessarily on offer to UK unions, but their pursuit may offer a better prospect of success for the future than lies in the attempt to re-establish a form of trade union power which emerged as a response to now-defunct employer strategies. The past success of decentralized bargaining by shop stewards relied upon a collusion between representatives and managers which suited particular market circumstances; the future successes of trade unions in the industry may rest on a similarly collusive basis, but those particular market circumstances are unlikely to return for some time. In particular, to the extent that trade union activity in the UK car industry is associated with restrictive practices it is unlikely to be able to protect either employment or earnings in the face of international competition.

NOTES

CHAPTER 3

1. Defined, after Pratten (1971:26) as 'the minimum scale above which any possible subsequent doubling in scale would reduce total average unit costs by less than 5%'.
2. There have been several recent descriptions of these processes: for example, CPRS 1975; Hartley 1981. This presentation relies heavily on Willman and Winch 1985.
3. This ceased to be the case after the new diesel engine plant came on stream at Dagenham in 1984.
4. The sources for this section are Abernathy *et al.* 1983 and Townsend *et al.* 1981, as well as those references.
5. Sources as for note 4, plus Jones (1981) and OECD (1983).
6. Except where indicated to the contrary, the sources for this section are: *Automotive Engineer* 1978–84, *British Business* 1984, *Engineer* 1980–84, *Engineering* 1980–84, and *Harvard Business Review*, 1975–84.
7. Managing Director (operators) Austin Rover Group.
8. Roger Smith, Chairman of GM, was quoted in 1983 as suggesting that a $1 per hour rise in wages would encourage a 10 per cent increase in the number of robots used by the Company (*Harvard Business Review*, May 1983).

CHAPTER 4

1. Sources for Figure 4. Output, measured in thousands of units:

Economic Trends; Employment, Department of Employment 'Employees in Employment', June figures. As far as possible, allowance was made for the changes in the Standard Industrial Classifications of 1948, 1958, 1968, and 1980. The employment series relates to the manufacture of motor vehicle and parts.

2. One final, albeit imperfect, indicator of the differences between the employment policies of companies in the different countries is given by the link between output and employment. The correlation coefficients ('r') indicate the extent to which employment follows changes in output, and the slope coefficients ('b') indicates the strength of the movements. The small number of observations (eleven in all) mean that small differences between countries are unlikely to be statistically significant.

Table 15 *The link between employment and output in the car industry in different countries, 1970–1980*

country	'r'	'b'
Japan	0.89	0.16
USA	0.89	0.41
UK	0.80	0.89
West Germany	0.60	0.57
France	0.44	0.17
Italy	0.04	0.04
Sweden	0.01	−0.19

Note: Year-on-year correlations using employment and output data from Streeck and Hoff (1983). Output measured in thousands of units, and employment in hundreds of workers.

Output changes affect employment most quickly in the USA, Japan, and the UK, and hardly at all in Italy and Sweden. In the USA the system of seniority rules for lay-offs left companies with a free hand in deciding the level of lay-offs. In Japan, the secondary labour force took the brunt of the adjustment to output changes. The weak correlation can be taken as evidence of greater employment security, except in Italy where the state lay-off compensation scheme leaves affected workers on the employer's books.

The slope coefficient indicates the size of the employment variation – thus in the UK a reduction in output of 1,000 units would lead to a reduction in employment of 89. The scale of output-related employment variations in the 1970s was then greatest in Britain, West Germany, and the USA, but small in the other countries. This would seem to be the result of employment policies and of productivity levels (employment fluctuations would be greatest where output per man was least).

3. Department of Employment New Earnings Survey 1976: the differential in average weekly earnings for manual men adults in Vehicles between those with 1–2 years' service and those with 10 or more years was 8.7 per cent, compared with 7.1 per cent for all manufacturing industry. The source for France, Italy, and West Germany was Eurostat SEI 1972, NACE 351, comparing those with less than 2 years' service to those with 10 or more years.

4. Earnings by occupation in engineering, shipbuilding, and chemicals, Department of Employment. The survey was discontinued after June, 1980.

5. Even before the major manpower reductions, the New Earnings Survey showed that in 1976, median length of service for all male manual adults in Vehicles was 9 years, compared with 6 years in Mechanical Engineering, and 7.5 years in manufacturing as a whole. This was after the car industry had lost its position at the top of manual workers' earnings league, and so is not simply the product of high relative wages. If one assumes that an organization has a fairly balanced service distribution, and that it is neither expanding nor contracting, doubling the median of current service gives a rough idea of what completed service would be. Thus one might expect median completed service to be between 15 and 20 years, a fair proportion of any workers' active working life. It is also interesting to compare this with results of the Japanese 1977 Basic Survey of Wage Structure (Japanese Yearbook of Labour Statistics 1977: Tables 79 and 83). The average length of current service of a male regular automobile assembler was 8.2 years (average age 33.4), and of male production workers in manufacturing establishments with 1,000 or more employees, 12.2 years. Thus although Japanese internal labour markets give longer service to their 'regular' work-force, it is not out of all comparison with Britain.

CHAPTER 6

1. These figures offer only a rough basis for comparison over time, due to the SIC change in 1980. Throughout this chapter, we shall use MLH 381 (SIC 1968) figures for the period up to 1982, and MLH 35 (SIC 1980) figures for 1983, except where specified.

2. That is, time allowances for changing in and out of work clothes.

3. Company figures; the calculation appears to assume 46-week working.
4. For example, in 1980, the percentages of total production in the first two quarters were: BL 55.6, Ford 58.6, Vauxhall 63.1, Talbot 73.2. The Talbot figure is inflated by the collapse of its market in the autumn. Similarly Vauxhall seasonal figures since 1982 have been masked by steady market growth.

CHAPTER 7

1. The inquiries were the work of the Joint Study Groups, consisting of the chief executives of the major firms and national union officials, established in the early 1960s under the auspices of the Ministry of Labour.
2. For differing views on the stewards role in the BL participation scheme see Alan Thornett's interview in the *Making Cars* television series and Derek Robinson interviewed in *Marxism Today*, 1980.
3. See the pamphlet 'What Happened at Speke?' by Huw Beynon (1980).

BIBLIOGRAPHY

Abernathy, W. J. (1978) *The Productivity Dilemma: Roadblock to Innovation in the Auto Industry*. Baltimore: Johns Hopkins.

Abernathy, W. J. and Wayne, K. (1974) Limits of the Learning Curve. *Harvard Business Review* 52(5): 109–19.

Abernathy, W. J., Clark, K., and Kantrow, A. (1983) *Industrial Renaissance*. New York: Basic Books.

Altshuler, A., Anderson, M., Jones, D., Roos, D. and Womack, J. (1984) *The Future of the Automobile: The Report of MIT's International Automobile Program*. London: Allen and Unwin.

Batstone, E. (1984) *Working Order*. Oxford: Blackwell.

Batstone, E., Boraston, I. and Frenkel, S. (1977) *Shop Stewards in Action*. Oxford: Blackwell.

Beynon, H. (1973) *Working for Ford*. Harmondsworth: Penguin.

—— (1977) *What Happened at Speke?* London: Transport and General Workers' Union.

—— (1984) *Working for Ford* (new edition). Harmondsworth: Penguin.

Bhaskar, K. (1979) *The Future of the UK Motor Industry*. London: Kogan Page.

Bloomfield, G. (1978) *The World Automotive Industry*. London: David and Clarke.

Brown, W. (1973) *Piecework Bargaining*. Oxford: Blackwell.

—— (ed.) (1983) *The Changing Contours of British Industrial Relations*. Oxford: Blackwell.

Brumlop, E. and Jurgens, U. (1983) *Rationalisation and Industrial Relations in the West German Motor Industry: A Case Study of*

Volkswagen. Discussion Paper DP83–216. Berlin: Internationales Institut für vergleichende Gesellschaftsforschung.

Central Policy Review Staff (1975) *The Future of the British Car Industry.* London: HMSO.

Dickson, K. and Fleck, T. (1984) Robotic Applications and Employment in the West Midlands. *West Midlands County Council Sector Report No. 5.*

Durcan, J., McCarthy, W. and Redman, G. (1983) *Strikes in Postwar Britain.* London: Allen and Unwin.

Edwardes, M. (1983) *Back from the Brink: An Apocalyptic Experience.* London: Collins.

Edwards, P. (1982) Britain's Changing Strike Problem. *Industrial Relations Journal* 13(2): 5–21.

Friedman, H. and Meredeen, S. (1980) *The Dynamics of Industrial Conflict.* London: Croom Helm.

Goldthorpe, J., Lockwood, D., Bechoffer, F. and Platt, J. (1968) *The Affluent Worker.* Cambridge: Cambridge University Press.

Grunberg, L. (1983) The Effect of Social Relations of Production on Productivity and Workers' Safety. *International Journal of Health Services* 13(4): 621–34.

—— (1984) Workplace Relations in the Economic Crisis: A Comparison of a British and French Automobile Plant. Paper to the ASA, mimeo. August, 1984.

Hartley, J. (1981) *Management of Vehicle Production.* London: Butterworth.

Hoff, A. (1983) Assessing Medium Term Investment-related Manpower Needs: A Case Study from the German Automobile Industry. In Streeck and Hoff (1983).

House of Commons (1975) *The Motor Vehicle Industry.* Fourteenth Report of the Trade and Industry Subcommittee of the Expenditure Committee. London: HMSO.

Hyman, R. (1983) Trade Unions: Structure Policies and Politics. In Bain, G. (ed.) *Industrial Relations in Britain.* Oxford: Blackwell.

Incomes Data Service Study (1981) Productivity Improvements. No. 245, July.

Jones, D. T. (1982) Technology and Employment in the UK Automobile Industry. (Paper given at Science Policy Research Unit, Brighton.)

Jones, D. T. (1983) Technology and the UK Automobile Industry. *Lloyds Bank Review* No. 148.

—— (1985) The Future of the Motor Industry in the UK Economy. Unpublished paper.

—— (1985) The Import Threat to the UK Car Industry. Science Policy Research Unit, University of Sussex.

Jones, D. T. and Prais, S. (1978) Plant Size and Productivity in the Motor Industry: Some International Comparisons. *Oxford Bulletin of Economics and Statistics* 40(2): 131–51.

Jones, D. T. *et al.* (1983) *The West Midlands Automobile Components Industry.* Report to the West Midlands County Council.

Katz, H. (1984) The US Automobile Collective Bargaining System in transition. *British Journal of Industrial Relations* 22(2).

—— (1985) *Shifting Gears: Changing Labor Relations in the US Auto Industry.* MIT Press.

Katz, H. and Karl, R. (1983) Personnel Planning in the US Automobile Industry. In Streeck and Hoff (1983) *Workforce Restructuring Manpower Management and Industrial Relations in the World Automobile Industry* 2.

Katz, H. and Streeck, W. (1984) Labor Relations and Employment Adjustments. Chapter 9 in Altshuler *et al.* (1984).

Lewchuck, W. (1983) Fordism and British Motor Car Employers. In Gospel, H. and Littler, C. (eds) *Managerial Strategies and Industrial Relations.* London: Heinemann.

—— (1984) The British Motor Vehicle Industry 1896–1982. The Route of Decline. Unpublished paper.

Malsch, T., Dohse, K. and Jurgens, U. (1984) Industrieroboter im Automobilbau: auf dem Sprung zum 'automatisierten Fordismus'? Discussion Paper DP84–217. Berlin: Internationales Institut für vergleichende Gesellschaftsforschung.

Manwaring, T. (1981) The Trade Union Response to New Technology. *Industrial Relations Journal* 12, 4.

Marsden, D. W. (1978) *Industrial Democracy and Industrial Control in West Germany, France and Great Britain.* Department of Employment Research Paper No. 4. London: Department of Employment.

—— (1980) Industrial Democracy, Job Regulation and Internal Labour Markets. In H. Diefenbacher and H. Nutzinger (eds). *Mitbestimmung: Probleme und Perspektiven der empirischen Forschung.* Frankfurt: Campus Verlag.

Maurice, M., Sellier, F. and Silvestre, J. J. (1978) *Production de la hierarchie dans l'entreprise: recherche d'un effet societal France–Allemagne.* Aix-en-Provence: LEST. Published as *Politique d'education et organisation industrielle en France et en Allemagne.* Paris: Presses Universitaires de France, 1982.

Maxcy, G. and Silbertson, Z. (1959) *The Motor Industry.* London: Allen and Unwin.

Melman, S. (1958) *Decision-making and Productivity*. Oxford: Blackwell.

OECD (1983) *Long-term Outlook for the World Automobile Industry*. Paris: OECD.

Owen, N. (1983) *Economies of Scale and Competitiveness in the EEC*. Oxford: Oxford University Press.

Passingham, B. and Connor, D. (1977) *Ford Shop Stewards on Industrial Democracy*. London: Institute of Workers' Control.

Peterson, W. (in collaboration with Forslin, B. and Forsberg, B.) (1983) Personnel Planning in the Swedish Automobile Industry. In Streeck and Hoff (1983).

Pratten, C. F. (1971) *Economies of Scale in British Manufacturing Industry*. Cambridge: Cambridge University Press.

Rhys, D. G. (1974) Employment, Efficiency and Labour Relations in the British Motor Industry. *Industrial Relations Journal* 5(2): 1–15.

Royal Commission on Trade Unions and Employers Associations. (Chairman: Lord Donovan). Report 1968 (Cmnd 3623).

Sabel, C. (1982) *Work and Politics*. Cambridge: Cambridge University Press.

Scarborough, H. (1984) Maintenance Workers and New Technology. *Industrial Relations Journal* 15(4): 9–17.

Streeck, W. (1984) *Industrial Relations in West Germany: A Case Study of the Car Industry*. London: Heinemann.

Streeck, W. and Hoff, A. (1982) Industrial Relations in the German Automobile Industry: Developments in the 1970s. Discussion Paper. Berlin: Internationales Institut für Management und Verwaltung.

Streeck, W. and Hoff, A. (eds) (1983) *Workforce Restructuring, Manpower Management and Industrial Relations in the World Automobile Industry*. Berlin: Internationales Institut für Management und Verwaltung.

Terry, M. (1983) Shop Stewards Through Expansion and Recession. *Industrial Relations Journal* 14(3): 49–58.

Tolliday, S. and Zeitlin, J. (1982) Shopfloor Bargaining, Contract Unionism and Job Control. Unpublished. Cambridge: King's College.

Townsend, J. *et al.* (1981) Science and Technology Indicators for the UK: Innovations in Britain Since 1945: Science Policy Research Unit, University of Sussex.

Turner, H., Clack, G. and Roberts, G. (1967) *Labour Relations in the Motor Industry*. London: Allen and Unwin.

Williams, K., Williams, J. and Thomas D. (1983) Why are the British bad at Manufacturing. London: Routledge and Kegan Paul.

Willman, P. (1984) The Reform of Collective Bargaining and Strike Activity at BL Cars. *Industrial Relations Journal* 15(2): 1–12.

—— (1985) Labour Relations Strategy at Austin Rover. In S. Tolliday and J. Zeitlin (eds) *Between Fordism and Flexibility*. Oxford: Oxford Policy Press.

Willman, P. and Winch, G. (1985) *Innovation and Management Control: Labour Relations at BL Cars*. Cambridge: Cambridge University Press.

NAME INDEX

SUBJECT INDEX

There is no separate heading for the British car industry as the book is written from that viewpoint (see p. 11).